✧ THE SUMMER OF LOVE ✧

THE SUMMER OF LOVE
Haight-Ashbury at its highest

Written and Photographed by
Gene Anthony

With Foreword by
Michael McClure

CELESTIALARTS
Berkeley, California

TO JILL

Faith creates; all else destroys.

Laurens van der Post

Concept and design by Jill Losson Anthony

*All photographs in this volume are
by Gene Anthony except for the following:
Bob Campbell, p. 31; Bill Ham archives p. 39;
Jim Marshall, pp. 40-41.*

Celestial Arts
P.O. Box 7327
Berkeley, California 94707

First Printing, January 1980

Library of Congress Cataloging in Publication Data

Anthony, Gene.
    The summer of love.

    Includes index.
        1. San Francisco—Social life and customs.
    2. Arts—California—San Francisco.
    3. Anthony, Gene.   I. Title.
    F869.S35A57   979.4'61053   79-52977
    ISBN 0-89087-250-3

Made in the United States of America

2   3   4   5   6   7   8—86

Contents ಜ

Spiritual Occasions 🙿

What is a spiritual occasion? Jackson Pollock swinging loops of paint making a splashing image in which appear the face and eyes of a perfect woman? No, not only Pollock but the whole spiral galaxy of abstract expressionists are a spiritual occasion. Rothko with his vibrant and mystical fields of red, orange, and blue; Clyfford Still creating erotic Blake-like wars of forces inherent in matter itself; Franz Kline slashing out calligrams for old feelings reborn in the skyscape and on tenement walls. That large moment in the history of art was a spiritual occasion giving depth to consciousness. It showed new combinations of sensation to senses that were weary with the old representations and the newer modernism alike. Those painters were heroes of a battle of liberation. They showed they could portray their spirits and the mammal movements of their bodies in the pain and joy and paint of consciousness that flowed from them.

Our lives seem like a thread on which we string births and deaths and marriages and sexual acts and feasts and all spiritual occasions. Our lives are strings of pearls that we look at and feel with the fingers of experience and remembrance. We are hungry for experience.

Stimulated by rock and roll, the poetry of the Beats, and a changed experience of Nature (felt directly with eyes and the soles of the feet) and through new drugs, a great hunger was created in the youth of America. To fill it they created their own spiritual occasion.

For them it wasn't necessary to have a paint brush in the hand and to leave an artifact in the form of a painting or sculpture. The event itself became both an organism and an artifact and had a brief life—but with the drugs there was no time, and to have any life, brief or long, was to exist forever in the uncarved block of time. The Fillmore and the Avalon Ballroom were ongoing rebirthing organisms. Each night a new creature came into existence. We were all part of it—our clothes of Billy the Kid and Jean Harlow and Saint Francis and Pied Piper and Tom O' Bedlam and Buddha and Daniel Boone and Robin Hood and Outlaw Cyclist were all ripples in the organism of the event, as well as expressions we'd longed for but feared to make. The costumes were not masks but were expressions—as were the stamping or light touch of the foot in the dancing—or the cry or moan of joy. A new tribe was coming into being. Anyone could scoff—could say it wouldn't last long, but those who believed in the Tribe knew in some secret place in their awareness that it didn't matter whether it lasted or not; a spiritual occasion has a set of laws other than the ones that extend the life of the one-dimensional society of car deals, factories, real estate, life insurance, and staging bases for bombs and napalm used to kill Asians in fishing villages.

Exuberance and intellectual and spiritual excitement cause love structures to come into being. More and more complicated associations of events and persons and organizations of matter join together. There were bigger dances, greater and greater joinings of hands reaching farther and farther until at last a Human Be-In was necessary to express the complication of feelings. The complex arrangements of sensations that created new experiences and a new belief in the body itself were the basis of it. Those parts and expressions of the body that were previously kept secret were there in public—the natural voice, the genitals, and the real aspirations that flesh consciousness makes, such as Hope. Hope was there and also the desire to define love. Love was an

abstraction to the Seekers. The Be-In was a spiritual occasion culminating from the countless preceding events, dances, thoughts, breaths, lovemakings, illuminations. The Be-In was a blossom. It was a flower. It was out in the weather. It didn't have all its petals. There were worms in the rose. It was perfect in its imperfections. It was what it was—and there had never been anything like it before.

Michael McClure

Thanks 🙰

My wife is primarily responsible for rediscovering my picture file of the Haight-Ashbury. The design of this book is a testimony of her talents and energy. Special thanks to Michael Bowen who gave me so much new information and many hours of interviews; I also sincerely thank Allen Cohen for his considerable efforts, his valuable research and his support; Bill Graham for his assistance and faith; Chet Helms who was most giving of his time and energies; and Michael McClure who found time to add to my manuscript. There were many people who were invaluable as I searched for new information concerning events that occurred during that Summer of Love. I would like to acknowledge the help and advice of my editor, David Morris; Jerry Kamstra; Mrs. Gladys Hanson, City Archivist, San Francisco Public Library; Peter Tamony; Peter and Judy Berg; Phyllis Willner; Jan Rassmussen; Ron Thelin; Jerry Mander; Bill Ham; Hank Harrison; Stewart Brand; Lenore Kandel; Gary Snyder; Peter Coyote; George Hunter; John Wong; O'Leary; and Satty. There were many other people, too, who offered bits of information, and of course, those in my pictures. To you where ever you may be: It's been a pleasure! I thank you one and all.

Preface

On reflection, my Haight-Ashbury experience was one of witnessing a twentieth-century Children's Crusade, a search by young people for consciousness and enlightenment. Certainly that mid-'sixties period was a psychic revolution with strong spiritual overtones. This book is a celebration of some of the events that occurred in and around the Haight-Ashbury, with new background information concerning the beginnings. This story is what I witnessed, the people I met and what I perceived to be happening. I emphasize that my story is only a small part of a larger history that covered many years. These are my recollections of key events that I feel started it all—a fifteen-month gestation period, November 1965 to mid-January 1967. I have tried to check my memory with the people who are part of this volume. I have focused on circumstance and people that I feel shaped that period that has been tagged "The Summer of Love" in the Haight-Ashbury, a movement that was like a fragile butterfly testing its wings for flight.

A Bouquet of Flowers 🌺

Jerry Garcia

During the mid-'sixties a phenomenon occurred in San Francisco that was to have a profound effect on America and the rest of the world. It was the emergence of a genuine counterculture; a vast segment of American youth, who openly declared ambitions counter to the prevailing American dream, that is, they stood in opposition to its ideals and the then current war in Vietnam. This counterculture had its focus and apotheosis in an area of San Francisco known as the Haight-Ashbury, the intersection of two streets whose very names soon became synonymous with the movement, and the people themselves.

In 1965 the "Hashbury" as the area was nicknamed, was a quiet neighborhood of ramshackle Victorian houses, empty storefronts and marginal businesses that was home to many blue- and white-collar workers, beatnik refugees who had fled the repression of North Beach, black families inching up from the Fillmore district ten blocks away, and Orientals moving in from the overcrowded ghetto of Chinatown. At the time the counterculture was forming, even before the kids themselves realized they were a counterculture, the rents in the Hashbury were cheap, available and open. The area was sunny, situated on the periphery of Golden Gate Park, a verdant expanse of open meadows, formal gardens, statuary and museums, one of the finest city parks in America. Haight Street became center stage for much of the action that was to take place for the next five years. The street begins at the eastern edge of Golden Gate Park and runs for 20 blocks through the Ashbury district, down through the Fillmore district, thence on to Market Street ten blocks away. Three blocks north, another green strip called the Panhandle parallels the Haight district for a mile. It was these miles of lush bordering parks, the cheap rents, and a neighborhood tolerant of students that was to start it all. Then there was rock'n'roll. And LSD.

In 1965 everyone was invited to the Hashbury. The area attracted a burgeoning procession of bearded and beaded jingle-jangling kids on foot, in psychedelic-painted VW vans, in cars, on motorcycles, in surplus mail trucks and those just riding the thumb. They came from all over America, and arrived to the scent of patchouli and musk incense and the beat of rock music that reverberated throughout the neighborhood of cavernous Victorian houses, harboring incipient rock and roll bands and the concomitant dopers, dealers and communalists.

For me it all began one day in the fall of 1965. My apartment was on Divisadero Street, one block up the hill from Haight Street. From my front windows I had a beautiful view of the city. During 1966, when the Haight got into high gear, not a day went by without a parade of strange apparitions headed into the Haight: kids wrapped in blankets or draped with flags or wearing antique clothes, cowboys and Indians, young girls with headbands of daisies, wearing their grandmothers' sleekysmoothies. And the feathers. And the ones blowing flutes and horns and bugles. And the dogs with the flowers tied to their collars. And the dancing . . . "with one hand waving free."

Every one was invited to the party
in the Hashbury

Psychedelic Rangerman 🌀

To get to the Hashbury from the corner of Divisadero and Haight, walk west past Buena Vista Park on the left, which faces a row of Victorian homes and apartment buildings. After four blocks you come to Masonic Avenue. At the intersection, stop. On the right corner, is the Drugstore Cafe. Since the turn of the century that gray, two-story building had been a drug emporium. The new owners kept the big brown glass bottles and a lot of other drugstore apparatus behind the glass cabinets as a reminder of the Cafe's beginnings. They kept the glass counters, too, and the mirrors, the big white free weighing machine, and the floor of little white octagonal tiles. The Drugstore Cafe was always loaded . . . one way or another.

Across the street on that corner was a head shop that sold a dozen varieties of colored rolling papers, ornate roach clips and clay, silver and brass hash pipes. Above one of the shops was the home of a painter, Michael Bowen. Michael's studio served as an early office for the San Francisco *Oracle*, the hip-

pie newspaper, a meeting place for itinerant writers, artists and photographers, and a crash pad for a succession of wandering American gurus.

Michael had received a certain notoriety when he was arrested during the headline-making LSD drug bust in Millbrook, New York, in 1965. (It was the now-famous raid on Tim Leary's Millbrook headquarters by G. Gordon Liddy. Liddy was then Assistant District Attorney in Poughkeepsie, New York, and out to build his reputation for his hop to the White House.)

Michael Bowen was an artist who lived his art. He helped create the Love Pageant Rally and the Human Be-In. Michael's stimulation came from his environment of friends, his guru, John Cooke, and a celebration of LSD.

(above) Martine, who lived with Michael, and Torah, asleep in their meditation room. (left) Macrobiotic meal at Bowen's place.

*Michael Bowen and his paintings.
His work reflected his voyages with
acid and the symbolism found in the
Hashbury.*

A lot was going on in Michael's place and it was always full of people. His flat was a reflection of the scene in the street. He often set up rolls of butcher paper or framed canvas on a big easel in the middle of his studio, and amid a nearly perpetual flow of milling friends, children and dogs, drew in charcoal or painted with oils a parade of Indians and cow-faced human figures dancing to baying wolves that were riding on the backs of wild-eyed stamped-ing horses and dancing clowns. Poet Allen Ginsberg dropped by Michael's place from time to time. So did LSD advocates Tim Leary and Dick Alpert, poet Gary Snyder, and Yippie leader Jerry Rubin. Some of the Hell's Angels dropped over, and a host of others, too.

"From the beasties and grumpies
        and things that go bump in the night,
                Dear Lord protect us."

"Revolution Evolution!
Evolution Revolution!"

Three heroes of the 'sixties visit the Hashbury. George Harrison and his new wife toured Haight Street; Dr. Timothy Leary, LSD's high priest; Captain Trips, Jerry Garcia of the Grateful Dead.

A Holy Man

One afternoon a wandering holy man, Charlie Brown, came by and explained to Michael and some friends the interesting relationship of the Pentagon Building in Washington to the wartime condition of the country from the point of view of a magical diagram. A magical diagram is an occult drawing put on the floor by a magician, who steps into it or concentrates on it. A pentagon encloses the design of a five-pointed star, which is the alchemical symbol for inverted power. That symbol, said Charlie Brown, is associated with war, murder, and apocalypse. It also happens to be, Bowen pointed out, the shape of the United States Army Medal of Honor, which is an inverted star. It was also noted by Charlie Brown that the Pentagon was built outside the mandala of Washington itself, on a swamp known as Hell's Bottom, and surrounded by five areas of pollution—a sewage treatment plant, two freeways, the polluted Potomac River, and a cemetery full of fallen war heroes. So it was decided on the spot by Michael Bowen that someone had to do something; someone had to put positive energy into his country's defense.

This was a situation that called for . . .

*Charlie
Brown*

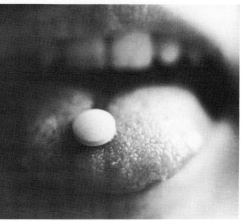

21

The Psychedelic Rangerman, Michael Bowen.

The Lone Psychedelic Ranger!

The Man in the White Hat 23

At that point, Michael became that man in the white hat. As a matter of fact, he was convinced part of his destiny during those years was connected with turning certain people on to LSD. Michael believed that by turning on enough individuals to lysergic acid diethylamide he would be acting for "the cause," for the enlightenment of humankind. Michael's quest was for greater psychic awareness in the world.

A young woman by the name of Martine was living with Michael Bowen at the time. She was acquainted with Jerry Rubin, then a student developing a name for himself as a radical political leader across the Bay at U.C. Berkeley. Michael suggested Rubin be invited to the studio so that Charlie Brown's disclosure about the symbolism of the Pentagon could be discussed. Jerry Rubin's first marijuana experience, and later his first LSD experience, was the result of that meeting with Michael. Rubin was given 1000 micrograms of Owsley's "White Lightning," and told of Charlie Brown's revelation. In the end, Rubin was one of the architects and developers of the March on the pentagon, and led his own psychedelic war against the linear, the fixed and the uptight.

Angels and Diggers 🌀

Live theater. That's what Haight Street was all about. Tourists the world over, from Europe to Japan, knew more about the Haight-Ashbury than they did about San Francisco. A survey made in 1968 in several parts of the Continent disclosed that more people knew the Haight-Ashbury was in California than knew the location of San Francisco. When tourists arrived in San Francisco, at the top of their list of sights to see was the Hashbury. Naturally, enterprising tour guides were quick to shepherd their charges out to see the hippies. Every hour, Gray Line tour buses journeyed out to the Haight from the downtown hotels—at six bucks a head. The tour was known as the "Hippie Hop" and was advertised as "a safari through psychedelphia, and the only foreign tour within the continental limits of the United States."

In the beginning, the kids on the street welcomed the packed tour buses with jovial, good-natured enthusiasm. Soon enough, the camera clicking straights became less welcome, and the Diggers and other groups started to use the legions of sightseers as players in games of their own. The Diggers were characterized by the San Francisco press as a "hippie philanthropic organization based in the Haight-Ashbury." For a time some of the tourist buses were met with crowds of mirror-toting hippies. The Diggers had salvaged a trash can filled with broken mirrors and passed them around to the kids on the street, who turned them on the occupants of the tour buses. Novelist Richard Brautigan ambled about the streets carrying a mirror that he held out before likely looking tourists, exclaiming, "Know thyself!"

The Diggers contributed a lot to the mystique that was so much a part of the Haight-Ashbury. If the Diggers had picked a key word to describe themselves, it would be *absurd.* It was an open organization. To announce oneself as a Digger was to be a Digger. As a matter of fact, to proclaim oneself a Digger was to be a founding member. A heavy hippie. A one percenter, as symbolized on the Digger poster. The poster depicts two Tong warriors leaning against a wall; below the black-suited Tongs is the symbol "1%" and the word *free.* The 1% symbol was borrowed from the Hell's Angels, another heavy fraternity that played a role in the Haight-Ashbury. The Hell's Angels wear a shoulder patch to proclaim their 1% status as bike riders. "Ninety-nine percent of all motorcyclists," says the American Motorcycle Association, "are decent, law-abiding citizens."

"We put '1%' on our poster," said Peter Berg, a founding member of the Diggers, "because we were saying that one percent of the people were willing to pull out all the stops to help change our society. The symbol was elitist. It was a challenge. It meant 'join us.' The poster," he said, "was designed to say 'see how heavy these Tong guys are.' The Tongs were known to wrap themselves with defensive chains. Well, you can be that heavy by being a Digger. Be free and do your own thing."

Diggers go far back in history. A large group of Diggers lived in the seventeenth century as an anarchistic communal farming group in Cromwellian England. Those early Diggers lived on waste lands that existed between the scattered countryside villages. They wanted the land to be free for all who needed to use it. Those ideological roots were reestablished by the Haight-Ashbury Diggers.

"We are all one!"

Weary arrivals responding to the new drum beat of 1966 landed daily in the Haight-Ashbury. (top) Writer Richard Brautigan carried his Digger mirror into the Panhandle and along the streets of the Hashbury treating hippies and tourists to a "free look."

The time has come to be free.

**** BE ****

**** FREE ****

Do your thing. Be what you are.

Do it.

NOW

This is our secret weapon.

This is how to do it

and it's groovy.

Printed by
the Communications Company

The Communications Company was the work of several writers including Richard Brautigan, Michael McClure, Lenore Kandel, Emmett Grogan, Peter Berg, and others. Communications were mimeographed on 8″ x 10″ sheets alerting hippies to events and free services.

Hell's Angels were the original One Percenters. They had a special rapport with the hippies. Their bridge of camaraderie had been established with a common interest — LSD.

A Digger design (right) was silk screened on posters and hand-size cards. To be a Digger was to be a heavy hippie and free.

The San Francisco contingent of the Diggers was born one night during a race riot in the Fillmore. Two young men, Emmett Grogan and Peter Berg, sat on a rooftop looking down into the streets filling with police and firemen battling with a crowd intent on burning up the Fillmore district. Emmett's friends became the nucleus of what became a large, informal group of people dedicated to a non-violent anarchy.

There were times in the Panhandle during peak traffic hours when the straights viewing the hippies were attracted by a 13-foot-high wooden frame. The Diggers set up the frame in front of their events as a portal through which Digger activity could be seen by the traffic-bound tourists and public. The frame was the "Digger Free Frame of Reference." The Diggers also had a store, "The Free Store." Everything was free. It started with free rides on a swing that hung from the rafters of the garage-front store on Page Street. Outside over the front doors stood a large wooden frame. The "clerks" rode around on roller skates. They were a free art show. To most of the straight world, a frame around almost anything is "Art."

Sculptor La Mortadella, Emmett Grogan, Slim Minnaux, Peter Berg, and Butcher Brooks on the steps of City Hall just moments after charges of creating a public nuisance were dropped in court. The five had put on some street theater and were arrested. They had all spent the night together in one jail cell. Grogan called it "a fun bust. The only time getting arrested had been a fun thing," he said. To Grogan the backward V gesture was meant to convey its English or Irish connotation: "Up your Ass."

Digger bean soup was legend.

*Phyllis Willner
in the Drugstore Cafe.*

Phyllis Willner was sixteen in 1966. She arrived in San Francisco cold and hungry from New York, riding on the buddy seat of a '62 Harley-Davidson. Penniless, she had nothing except the clothes on her back, a thin, black leather jacket and a purple dress. At Tracy's, a coffee and doughnut shop on Haight St., Phyllis stopped to answer a call of nature. Inside the bathroom, a notice pasted to the wall caught her eye. The words were in the design of a falling snowflake: FREE FREE FREE FOOD FOOD FREE FOOD FREE TODAY AT THE PANHANDLE AT 4:00 P.M.

It was a place to go. Phyllis was alone and starving. So she asked directions to the Panhandle.

The Diggers fed hundreds of hungry people under the tall eucalyptus trees in the Panhandle. Phyllis met Emmett Grogan there. Peter Berg and Judy and Peter Cohon. Grogan had started a free food project. He was a visionary and an experienced player in the sometimes lethal game of ringalevio that originated on the lower east side of Manhattan, where he grew up. His free meals had become daily ritual for the hungry in the Haight-Ashbury, and his charismatic personality attracted people who could help keep the program going. Grogan had friends in the San Francisco Mime Troupe, too; they were his partners. It was a brotherhood. Some of the Mime Troupe became Diggers— guerrilla fighters performing guerrilla theater.

During the Summer of Love the Digger Free Food truck could be counted on to arrive in the Panhandle at 4 P.M.

Phyllis Willner's destiny was to serve. Each day, every day, Phyllis and Judy and Nina and Julie and Mona searched for food and then cooked it. (Grogan had even been arrested and jailed for stealing meat for the free food cause.) Sometimes the food was cooked in milk cans over open fires. or at the Presbyterian church kitchen on Waller Street. Wherever a kitchen space could be found. But everyday there was cooking to be done for hungry people.

The Digger women were up and out at dawn searching the produce market stalls, the chicken slaughterhouses, the fish docks and the bakeries. The girls could be very seductive: Little Sisters of Christ accepting all offers of food and charity. Ripe produce, chicken wings, and two-day-old sourdough bread. The cooks could do a lot with that. It made a fair menu.

The Diggers made the produce pickups in a '58 Dodge truck that had been provided by a rich lady friend of Richard Brautigan. Each week Phil, at the chicken warehouse, was good for two cases of chicken wings. Ray, at the fish dock, provided a box of fish. And so it went. One day the Diggers received a message. A marine biologist from the Fish and Game Department was offering a whale that had been illegally caught by some fishermen. The carcass was stripped and the meat filled the Dodge truck. "We pounded the shit out of that meat," said Phyllis, "but it wasn't bad at all. It was OK and lasted a long time."

The Digger free meal in the Panhandle provided more than just something to eat. The gathering of hippies was a place for people in similar plight to work on some of their more urgent needs and problems. Phyllis Willner found some new friends there and a whole new life for herself.

George Hunter, leader of the Charlatans, strikes a pose next to Mike Wilhelm and Jerry Garcia.

The Red Dog Gang

The Charlatans.

Until the late 'fifties, San Francisco State College had its campus in close proximity to two traditionally low-rent districts: the Fillmore, which was largely populated by blacks, and the Haight-Ashbury, which had a mix of white and Oriental ethnic groups. In the late 'fifties, S.F. State moved its campus out to 19th Avenue, not far from the ocean. The new campus had few facilities for housing students, so they stayed in the Haight, where rooms and apartments were cheap.

Rodney Albin, a psychology major at S.F. State, had an uncle who owned a big old house at 1090 Page Street. The house had once been a grand mansion with whistle communication tubes connecting twenty-eight hardwood paneled and leather- and paper-walled rooms. "Ten-Ninety," as the old house was lovingly called by a long list of residents, had been a workingman's boardinghouse during the 'forties and 'fifties. Before that, 1090 had been a rich man's home, complete with a parquet-floor ballroom in the basement. Over the years the old house had become somewhat derelict. A lot of different people hung out there, including musicians, students and dope dealers.

The ballroom in the basement of 1090 Page had a little stage with Ionic columns. The room made an excellent rehearsal room and a good place to jam. Rodney started a rock group there—The Liberty Hill Aristocrats.

About this time some other S.F. State students and musicians started to hang out at 1090. Mike Wilhelm, Dan Hicks, Mike Ferguson, Richie Olsen, and George Hunter. Ferguson was the proprietor of the first San Francisco head shop: The Magic Theatre for Mad Men Only. The shop was down the street from 1090 on Divisadero Street. It was the first place to sell a variety of rolling papers and hash pipes for the express purpose of smoking dope—which was also sold, along with antiques and things.

George Hunter was the original Charlatan. He gets credit for helping develop much of the Victorian motif in the hippie domain. Maxfield Parrish was George's guiding light. George wasn't exactly a musician, although he learned to play the tambourine. George's talent was more visual—he was the archetypal showman. George and his partners liked to parade about as musicians at San Francisco Airport and the downtown hotels with empty instrument cases under their arms. Most of the boys didn't even own an "ax."

The Charlatans were the first psychedelic band. Before rock there was the angry sound of John Coltrane and Ornette Coleman. They were the squeak, honk and howl sound. Then, The Mystery Trend; Paul Revere and the Raiders, who emulated Liverpool rock; Doug Sahn became Sir Douglas because it was the thing to be English. The Beau Brummels were very western European, even though they came out of S.F. State.

The Charlatans were very American, sort of like cowboys—all dressed up wearing guns, riding horses, and going up to Virginia City to be rock 'n' roll stars. That was where the Charlatans had their first paid job.

There was a man in that Sierra foothill city named Mark Inobsky who owned a three-story red brick building on the main street of town. The place had a century-old handcarved and paneled bar that had come around Cape Horn in 1850. Upstairs over the bar were two floors of "rooms." Inobsky had envisioned opening a club with a western saloon atmosphere. His vision also included a French restaurant and a live band. But the entertainment had to be "different," something that the gamblers and tourists would remember, a memorable watering hole on the road to Reno and Carson City in Nevada.

Inobsky had a sidekick, a run-into-town-to-get-whatever-is-needed associate called Chandler "Travis T. Hip" Laughlin. Mr. "Hip" was sent to the Bay area to look for talent. His search led him to Bill Ham.

Bill Ham –
The Light Show Man.

Bill Ham managed rooming houses for itinerant musicians at 2111 and 1836 Pine Street, on the slope of the hill above "Jimbo's Bop City." Several of Ham's tenants worked at the jazz club on the edge of the Fillmore district. Ham was an artist, a painter, who in effect was experimenting with methods of plugging his painting into the wall—into the electrical current as musicans were doing with their guitars. Ham had an Army surplus light apparatus which was used by the military to project training materials onto large screens. He used it in the basement of "Pine Street." Ham introduced watercolor pigments that, when projected with oil solutions, resulted in fascinating wall-sized landscapes. By manipulating the liquids with the rhythms of music, Ham could create surging, pulsating effects that were downright psychedelic. Psychedelic lights. The whipped cream and the cherry for a rock 'n 'roll show. Ham introduced Mr. "Hip" to George Hunter and the rest of the Charlatans. The result of that chemistry was the first psychedelic rock 'n 'roll show. It was show time at the Red Dog Saloon in Virginia City.

The summer of '65 in Virginia City for the Charlatans was too good to last. It was every day, every night, a two-month movie. The band lived with the crew of the Red Dog above the saloon in the "rooms." By the end of the summer, things at the bar were getting pretty outrageous. The Charlatans had started to believe their own image, including the toting of guns. Stopping for gas one night on their way into the Bay area, the Charlatans were spotted by a cruising police car. The boys looked too freaky to be legal. In the process of checking them out, the police spotted the guns. Then they found some of the dread weed, marijuana! Dope!

That was the end of the line—the saga of the Charlatans at the Red Dog Saloon.

The Charlatans 1966: George
Hunter, Mike Wilhelm, Mike
Ferguson, Dan Hicks, Richie Olsen,
posed for the publicity photo on the
following page.

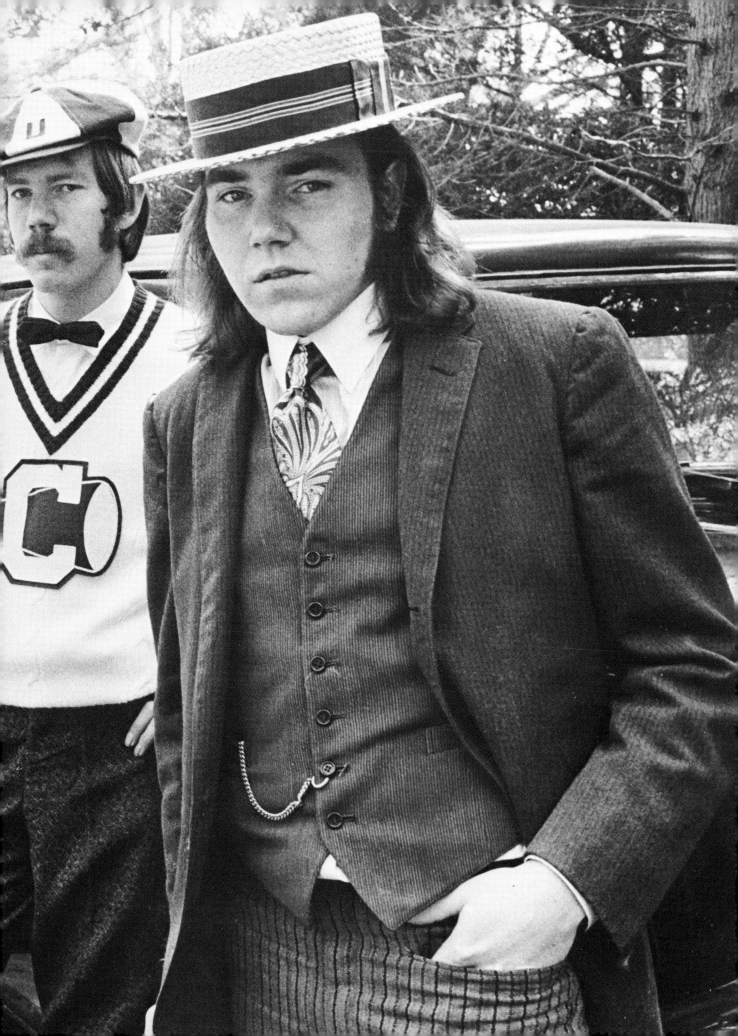

Seven-Ten Ashbury ☙

Spilling from the Grateful Dead headquarters at 710 Ashbury Street: three Charlatans, Jim Gurley, Mountain Girl with her baby Sunshine and Michael Bowen.

When the Charlatans returned to San Francisco from Virginia City, they were looked upon with a special reverence by their Bay area contemporaries. The Charlatans, after all, had worked a summer-long gig. Not many musicians as new to music as these lads could say the same. Putting a group together took time and money and a lot of initiative and energy. Besides, most of the younger musicians had been schooled in jazz and folk, so when the boys came to town from the Red Dog Saloon up in the country, there were lots of folks who wanted to share in their glow. And 1090 was the place to hang out. Janis Joplin came by, and a group calling itself the Warlocks (later to become The Grateful Dead) from Palo Alto. Big Brother and the Holding Company was formed at 1090 and so was the third Family Dog. Early in 1966 a lot of the local rock band social action moved three blocks west to The Grateful Dead's headquarters at 710 Ashbury.

Jerry Garcia.

The Grateful Dead returning calls on the front porch of Seven-Ten. Jerry Garcia, Pigpen, Phil Lesh, Bill Kreutzmann, and Bob Weir. Part of the fun of forming a band was the group energy. A visitor to the Grateful Dead house could "feel" it.

Pigpen — Ron McKernon

The Grateful Dead was the center band. Their music was equated with the LSD experience. They were the rock 'n 'roll group that other musicians went out of their way to hear and study. In the fall of 1965 the band was called The Warlocks, when Jerry Garcia changed the name to Grateful Dead, a name taken from a translation of an Egyptian tomb inscription. Bill Kreutzmann was the drummer, Bob Weir played rhythm guitar, Phil Lesh, bass, and Pigpen electric organ. LSD entrepreneur Owsley Stanley III was the financial backer for the group. Their headquarters was in a Victorian at 710 Ashbury Street. It was a unique group with a unique aura. The boys enjoyed their work. They were primarily into rock music for the fun of it all. Music was their art and it gave them pleasure. That enjoyment was communicated to their fans. An all-American success secret.

Inside the Grateful Dead house on a Sunday afternoon.

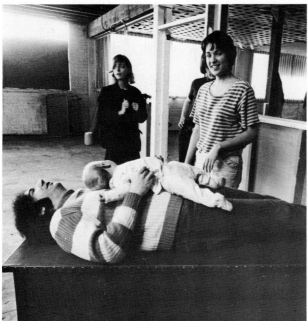

(top) Jerry Garcia, Danny Rifkin, and Burt Kanegson, later manager for the group.

(lower right) Grateful Dead practice session in a south of Market warehouse.

Jerry Garcia, Sunshine, Mountain Girl take a break from rehearsal with the band.

The Grateful Dead, 1966.

Poster artist Mouse.

Mountain Girl who lived at Seven-Ten.

Danny Rifkin,
manager of the Grateful Dead.

Jerry Garcia and Sunshine.

The Grateful Dead, 1966.

The Family Dog 🐾

Chet Helms

The First Family Dog company was formed at the "Dog House," the rooming house at 1836 Pine Street managed by Bill Ham. The "Dog House" developed its name from the fact that each of the house's dozen residents owned a dog. For a while Michael Bowen shared a small room there with a Great Dane. Four of the "Dog House" residents formed the first Family Dog company. It was a dope marketing enterprise until the company changed hands. George Hunter and Rock Scully (later manager of The Grateful Dead) became the second proprietors of The Family Dog until its third owner, Chet Helms, took over the leash.

Rock Scully, road manager for the Grateful Dead.

"May the Good Lord Shut Your Mouth
and
Open Your Mind."

The Avalon Ballroom Motto

Michael Bowen with Torah.

Big Brother and The Holding Company had been the last two names on a long list of rock band name suggestions that Chet Helms had been considering for a new rock group. Helms was the manager of a band without a name. Every name the Family Dog "family" could think of had been added to a list. The names were read aloud for the umpteenth time. The last two names read together had a special appeal to Chet Helms. That was it! Big Brother and the Holding Company. Show time!

For those with the munchies the fudge goodies at the food bar in the Avalon were extra special.

Light show artists at the Avalon. The mood that the light show people created with their color projections pulsing in time with the rock rhythms was one of dancing in a celestial dimension. The rock 'n 'roll music and the light display was an assault on the senses few would forget.

Chet organized weekend jam sessions at 1090. It got to be public. Chet had 50-cent Wednesday night jam sessions with Janis Joplin and Big Brother and the Holding Company. It all lasted twenty weeks—twenty weeks of future international rock stars. But Chet's real interest was playing music, not promoting it. Yet, as he said, "There are plenty of musicians around, and little venue. I ended up providing the venue."

Chet's first Fillmore Auditorium concert was February 19, 1966, starring The Jefferson Airplane and Big Brother and the Holding Company, at two dollars per ticket. It was announced by a black and white poster, the first in a long series of poster works by Wes Wilson. Wilson followed with the next weekend's attraction: A King Kong Memorial Dance poster that headlined The Great Society, Grass Roots, Big Brother and the Holding Company, and Quicksilver Messenger Service. Toward the end of April, Chet Helms left the Fillmore Auditorium solely to Bill Graham, and opened up the Avalon Ballroom at Sutter Street and Van Ness Avenue with The Blues Project, The Great Society, with "lights and stuff" by Tony Martin. "May the baby Jesus shut your mouth and open your mind" was the motto around the Avalon.

Chet Helms, a poet with a family background in the ministry, hails from Austin, Texas. Early on he had aspirations of being a musician. His lady friend, Janis Joplin, had been attending summer school at the University of Texas. Eager to get out to the West Coast music scene, Chet talked Janis into dropping her summer history classes and hitchhiking with him to San Francisco. It took them fifty hours.

For weeks and months and years, a weekend in San Francisco was taken seriously by a devoted following of fans who were considered "family" at the Avalon. Bill Ham, the light show man, made his debut at the Avalon, too.

Initiation 🎵

Rock music impresario Bill Graham's initiation into live music was at the Calliope Warehouse, known as "The Loft." It was an old horse and buggy stable south of the San Francisco *Chronicle* Building that had been turned into a hotel, later a pie factory, then a flop house. In 1965 most of the old building in the inner Mission district was used as office and rehearsal space for the San Francisco Mime Troupe. Bill Graham had worked there as business manager since 1964, but the job was wearing thin on him and he told Ronnie Davis, founder and director of the Mime Troupe, that he wanted to go on alone to other activities.

However, as a parting gesture of goodwill, Graham wanted to manage a benefit party for the Mime Troupers. He called it Appeal I. The benefit would attempt to raise badly needed funds, using the talents of various people from the City and down the Peninsula. Bill telephoned all the entertainers he could think of, artists and cinematographers and performers. The Jefferson Airplane, recently formed in August and using the Loft for rehearsal space, said they would be there. Someone else knew Frank Zappa (The Mothers of Invention). During this planning period, Chet Helms called and announced himself as leader of The Family Dog. Chet wanted to lend a hand at the benefit. "Fine," said Bill, "and will you please bring the dog act, too, because I think we can use it." It was fall of 1965; Graham was so unfamiliar with the music business that he had yet to become conscious of the Mersey beat from the Cavern Club in Liverpool, England.

The Mime Troupe handbill for November 6, 1965, advertises: "Appeal I (for continued artistic freedom in the arts). The Jefferson Airplane, the Fugs, Sandy Bull, the John Handy Quintet, The Committee actors, poet Lawrence Ferlinghetti, The Family Dog, The Warlocks, and others." The benefit would be Graham's introduction into rock show biz.

Bill Graham in his office at the Fillmore had just been informed that his Dance Hall Permit to Operate was permanent and no longer an issue of possible revocation with the cops.

and raisins and whistles and clicking noisemakers and little mirrors all individually wrapped in Christmas gift papers. And there was a thundering din of rock 'n 'roll that beat against the walls, echoing across the alleys like a beacon. The place was wall-to-wall straight and groovy Goodwill-party-costumed kids. Jugs of booze and "orange barrel" Kool-Aid were dispensed from garbage cans lined with aluminum foil—strange concoctions that were all things to all people.

Around midnight Graham had his introduction to the "Blue Meanies." "Too much noise," they said. "No permit and no fire exit." It was a nightmare of violations. A party of over fifty people in an art studio constituted a commercial enterprise. But Graham cajoled his adversary, a sergeant, by calling him "Captain" and clearing out half the crowd. The party rolled on. The promised attendance was reduced, but those who left by the front door were replaced by the tail end of the line of people who were fed up a back freight elevator. When the dawn arrived Allen Ginsberg, who was there exploring America on a Guggenheim Poetry Fellowship, chanted a mantra—a prayer for the new day to come.

It was Ralph Gleason, the jazz critic for the *Chronicle,* who suggested to Bill Graham that he check out a second-floor facility at Geary and Fillmore Streets called the Fillmore Auditorium. It was a good place to hold future benefits—a ballroom that had been used for decades as a dance hall.

The success of the November 6 benefit was quickly communicated. Those who had attended Appeal I deluged Graham and the Mime Troupe with phone calls and mail, imploring them to produce a second edition of the same menu, so there was a second Appeal, and a third. too, at the Fillmore Auditorium.

The price of a ticket for Appeal I was set according to one's ability to pay; it was a "donation." At the top of the stairs, as one entered the Loft, there was a 4' x 8' piece of sheetrock. On it was handpainted a sign: "Donation: Unemployed, small change; part-time job holder, 39 cents; full-time job holder, 89 cents . . ." The list went on to detail reduced rates for families with one child, and two parents living together. Various age groups were charged still another set of tolls. It was a long list.

And so was the line of people that waited to get in for the benefit. It stretched around the block and up the alley.

Inside the warehouse a new world was unfolding. Films flickered on walls. Bunches of grapes, tangerines, apples and sticks of gum hung on strings suspended from the rafters; There were gifts of coins

A Dream of Rainbows 23

Allen Cohen and photographer Ed Shea on Haight Street.

Allen Cohen sold LSD—"orange sunshine," "blue barrels," "white lightning" (a legal substance until October 6, 1966) for the now-famous Augustus Owsley Stanley III. Owsley made the best acid. An Owsley tab was the finest acid around. "Everyone saw LSD," said Cohen, "as being the opening to the unity of mankind, the wholeness of being, the means for developing and expanding human consciousness, and an increase of intelligence and compassion. We put everything into projections with LSD. The more positive a person's conditioning to LSD, the better his trips. Your expectations often determine what you explore in your mind on your trips."

There was a lot of loose money around the Haight-Ashbury. People were living on the proceeds from selling LSD or grass. People didn't need much money because many of them were living communally. Rents for rooms with kitchen privileges were often twenty or thirty dollars a month. Food wasn't all that expensive. Hippies lived like Bohemians have always lived—simply. So it wasn't very difficult to buy a little grass, sell a little, smoke a little, and have your month's rent, too. In those days grass was going for ten to fifteen dollars a lid. There were no big truckload importers. Grass came over the border stashed under the back seat of the family car. Once in the United States, in 1965, a kilo of Acapulco Gold sold for eighty dollars.

While Allen Cohen was dealing, he met the Thelin brothers, Ron and Jay, two dropouts from a parking lot, boat and umbrella rental business at Lake Tahoe. Allen turned the brothers on to some of Owsley's acid. Later the brothers opened up the Psychedelic Shop.

One night a few months after the Psych Shop had opened for business, Allen Cohen had a prophetic dream. In his dream, he saw a newspaper with rainbows on it. He mentioned the dream to a lady with whom he was living at the time. She told several friends, who told the Thelin brothers. A few days later while Allen was walking down Haight Street he met Ron Thelin, who said, "Hey, I hear that you had a dream about a newspaper with rainbows on it. Let's do it." Essentially Allen's idea was to create a newspaper that would express the feelings developing in the Haight-Ashbury.

Allen Ginsberg

One kilo (2.2 lbs.) of quality grass
sold for eighty dollars in 1966.
(following page)

55

The Oracle 23

Allen Cohen, editor of the San Francisco Oracle.

The name San Francisco *Oracle* was developed after a series of meetings. There was a small group of people involved at first, and everyone had an idea for the name. Ron Thelin wanted it *Psychedelic Oracle.* Someone else wanted *Psychedelic Oracle Frisco.* There were power plays, and more meetings. A Progressive Labor Party person argued for a Labor Party newspaper. Ron Thelin had the money, and he decided that the Labor Party people knew more about running a paper. *P.O. Frisco* came off the presses in August.

To the dismay of Allen Cohen and Ron Thelin, the first issue was terrible. The lead story was an article that the Progressive Labor Party had published several times in the past in other underground papers, about the camps which had been used to incarcerate Japanese during World War II, and they were being kept in readiness for revolutionaries and Bohemians. The second article described how groovy masturbation is. With that issue most of the staff decided to do other things with their time, but Allen persevered because of his vision. By the third issue, he was the editor. And on September 9, 1966, the paper had changed names and was out on the street. The San Francisco *Oracle* was finally issuing proclamations and declarations from the Haight-Ashbury.

Gabe Katz, a painter who signed his work "Anonymous Benefactor," drove out to the Haight-Ashbury from New York about the time the first *Oracle* hit the street. Katz had worked as a graphic

The art director of the Oracle, Steve Levin, who designed flowing bodies of text for the Haight-Ashbury paper instead of traditional columns.

Hawking the Oracle on Haight Street.

artist in New York, and knew Michael Bowen. When Katz arrived in San Francisco, he "crashed" at Bowen's. Then Bowen turned Katz on to the *Oracle*. Katz helped Allen Cohen manifest his vision of a newspaper with rainbows on it. The idea was workable; it had potential. The trick was to introduce different colored inks into the ink fountains on the printing press. The process is known as "split fountain." Colors meld together, causing a rainbow effect. With the sixth issue, after infusions of money from various benefactors—including Bill Graham of the Fillmore, Alex Geluardi, Peter Tork of the Monkeys, The Grateful Dead, and various marijuana dealers—the San Francisco *Oracle* was sputtering along in spasms of crisis. But the paper was a living force. As each issue came off the press, it was sprayed with jasmine perfume. Printing it was the biggest hassle: A complete issue of the *Oracle* required several print runs, i.e. first a fraction of the intended run was printed, these sold on the street, money collected, bills paid, and then a larger print run was ordered, until the total was completed. The largest total run of a single issue of the paper was 117,000. Then, after twelve issues, the romance began to pale and Allen Cohen's dream started to fade.

"The *Oracle*," said Allen, "was an attempt to break the lie of our linear habit. It was a contrast to regular papers, intended to show that most newspapers' objectivity was ugly and a lie. The *Oracle* was a judo on the newspaper format. It became a vehicle for information and the growing interests that were evolving in the Haight. We tried to include as much as we could. We didn't want to get involved in the day-to-day events, as Max Scheer, publisher of the *Berkeley Barb*, does. Mostly we were interested in subjective reportage generating poetic, philosophic ideas in a newspaper format. For example, when Super Spade, the drug dealer, was murdered in the Haight, I wrote an article that was called 'In Memorial.' It was a poetic invocation of some of the forces that were involved in the crime."

No one made any money from the *Oracle*. Sometimes in an emergency one of the staff could get rent money, but nothing else. But for their efforts, the *Oracle* became known as an important innovation in newspaper publishing that was imitated by magazines and alternative newspapers around the country.

The Psych Shop 23

T he Thelin brothers had opened up the Psychedelic Shop at 1535 Haight Street with the proceeds of their Tahoe business on January 1, 1966. At the start, the shop sold books and records and magazines. "My brother and I," said Ron, "had some strong feelings about the things that were happening on Haight Street. We didn't have any language for what was happening, but we knew that a whole new world was opening up. We wanted to be a part of it."

The Psychedelic Shop was a well-known refuge for street people. After a few months, the brothers expanded their operation to include a meditation room. A lot of lovemaking went on within its darkened interior. "Quite possibly a number of babies were conceived there," says Ron.

When the Straight Theater several blocks west on Haight Street expanded their activities, two front rows of folding seats had to be removed to make room for a stage. Three of those seats found

Police checked ID's on Haight Street against a growing list of runaways.

60

their way to the Psych Shop. "We set them in the shop front," said Ron. "Our window was a live display of whoever was sitting there looking out at the people looking in on them. It blew a lot of minds. Our display was a kind of mirror image of the street action outside." The Psychedelic Shop was also the first store on the street to put up a community bulletin board for people to leave messages. It was the forerunner of the Hip Switchboard. "The Psych Shop," says Ron, "was a center for a Haight-Ashbury communications network. It was a focus of attention for the press, too. A common expression in the Haight was, 'I'll meet ya at the Psychedelic Shop.'"

Jay Thelin owned the Psychedelic Shop with his brother Ron at 1535 Haight Street.

The Straight Theatre put on programs that involved the whole Hashbury community.

The Psychedelic Shop developed as a reading center and a popular Hashbury meeting place.

The drama and the spirit of the Haight-Ashbury captured the imagination and fantasies of millions of people around the world. Young people, dropouts and seekers of a change of lifestyle, poured into the Hashbury with increasing frequency during the spring of '66. The police in San Francisco made 8831 contacts with juveniles during the first six months of the year, a whopping increase over the previous year. Twelve hundred thirty-one teens under sixteen had been reported as runaways in San Francisco. Thousands more were soon to be on the march to join the legions of flower children.

The *Oracle* and the Psychedelic Shop received handfuls of letters daily from kids all over the country asking for guidance in their desire to get to the Haight. A young woman in New York poured out her desperate plea in a letter to the *Oracle:*

Dear Oracle *People,*

This is a plea for help.

I am being held a prisoner. I am the prison that holds me captive and I can't seem to escape myself.

Up until a few months ago when I took my first trip, I thought there was no reason to be alive and was about to settle on merely existing . . . trying to get by the next fifty years or so that way. But I saw that there is more.

But New York City is an awful place. The Lower East Side cannot be believed as to what it does to human dignity and freedom. It seems everyone is looking West and all anyone talks about here is when they are leaving for the Coast.

I am afraid. What if it isn't as it seems . . . as acid has shown me life ought to be. I've heard so much . . . read so much. Your paper is beautiful, beautiful, beautiful. But because I'm not just stifled by the environment but most of all by my self . . . it is a very hard thing to summon the courage to act and come there. Like anyone, I've been stepped on a lot and have reacted by learning the futility of my words and rarely find the courage to do more than smile at a friendly face.

If I would come, it would be alone. And I would probably never lift my eyes from the sidewalk . . . and how does one make friends or get help if no one can see the plea in your eyes because you are looking down.

The Love Rally here on Easter Sunday was a beautiful thing. All the uptightness in everyone was gone. No need for words . . . people just standing together — loving each other — doing their own thing. No one could believe it was really happening. But for New York the love rally ended at sundown.

I know people are trying here. The League for Spiritual Discovery is finally open, there's the Peaceeye Bookstore, and a group called the Jade Companions. But they are used by only a select few. I know it's not their fault. I've never been to any of these places other than to walk by and look in hoping for . . . something.

But I am my own prison and can't escape from myself enough to find what the rally promised there could be here. I know most of the problems are in my own head. But I also know that I need help. And you are the voice of the place I feel it should be.

If someone has read this far — please, please could someone, would someone, take the time to write me and tell me the right things so I won't be afraid to come to San Francisco. Please . . . something concrete — a name, address — something to come to. I need direction and I think maybe I could give a lot if someone would help me . . . or even better, need my help. Thank you.

Love,

V.M.

NYC

The kids kept coming. There were more of them every day. They arrived in cars and vans and on motorcycles and down at the Seventh Street Greyhound Bus terminal. With bed rolls and dark, dusty suitcases from all across the country. The new ones had a wide-eyed, bewildered, lost look in their eyes. And their clothes had a certain patina.

Bare feet on Haight Street came in two classes: clean bare feet belonging to the young ones that had gone into the Haight for an afternoon's adventure, leaving their shoes and socks in their mom's car down the street, and the dirty feet that had really been down on their luck. But during '66 it was rare to find desperately poor feet. When things got to be too weird there was always a variety of helping hands.

Alternate Paths

Leary advocated LSD as a liberator of social hang-ups. His slogan, "Turn On, Tune In, Drop Out," captured the attention of the media who made Leary a hippie star.

There was even a secret school. "The mystery school." "The six-day school." You could only go for six days. Everything was provided—meals, a place to sleep, even transportation. All you had to do was know that you would be gone for six days. The six-day school bus departed from the Panhandle. The school was run by Ambrose Hollingsworth and several psychics, magicians and teachers in an old Petaluma Victorian mansion. There were palmists and people who taught spiritual healing. Rhythm class was simply running and jumping. Spiritual healing was taught by an elderly couple who tutored their charges about the archangels and how to write letters to them.

Tim Leary's League for Spiritual Discovery was headquartered in a 46-room mansion at Millbrook, New York. Millionaire Billy Hitchcock owned the building that was known to the hippies as Millbrook.

(top) Tim Leary and Billy Hitchcock took part in Eastern dance instruction with members of the household at Millbrook.

"Divine substance is doing its perfect work in your mind, your body and all your affairs.**"**

From a letter to an archangel

"Each one must seek out the unique meaning in himself.
If I don't do it, who will do it?
If I don't do it now, when will I do it?
If I only do it for myself,
then what value will it have?**"**

From the archangel's answer

Tim Leary "through the looking glass."

The Free Clinic

It was always busy and never closed to anyone needing help.

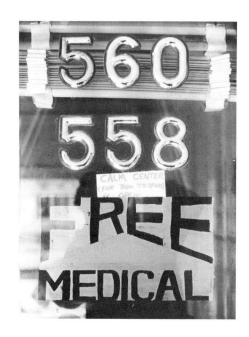

Dr. David Smith, founder of the Haight-Ashbury Free Clinic, and associates.

The waiting room at the Free Clinic in the Haight-Ashbury remained open around the clock. (bottom left) A Calm Center in the Free Clinic was specially set up for psychedelic space pilots who needed help in finding their way back down to earth.

Hippie Hill 🌀

F or someone who had been on the road, traveling to San Francisco to join the legions of flower folk, the best place to get some bearings was from the top of a small hill in Golden Gate Park, "Hippie Hill," a sloping green lawn just off Kezar Drive. From the Hill there is an uninterrupted view extending a thousand feet to a children's playground at the other end. On either side of the lawn are stands of eucalyptus and oak. It's a huge meadow, a quiet place away from the pervasive sound of the city. One could get stoned just by sitting in the right place. Someone would pass a "J" your way soon enough. The Hill was free from dope arrests. Out of sight, out of mind of Park Police Station, which could be seen from the top of Hippie Hill. It was a place to score a variety of things; a roommate, a pad, a lid, a friend. It was also a good place to spend a few hours just watching the show.

Hippie Hill in Golden Gate Park (preceding page)

Wilhelm Joerres was a handsome tall blond
man who had a passion for wearing snakeskin
boots with matching jacket, topcoat and hat.
Wilhelm was no simple clothes hound. His act
included a classic Jaguar sedan avec slinky
ladies for added flash. Wilhelm had a sense of
humor, too. He held office hours on Hippie
Hill and he ran for San Francisco Mayor. If
elected, he addressed the multitudes on the
hill, he would legalize the sale of pure narcotics
and encourage the "proper" use of LSD. He
would allow prostitution as a "necessary evil."
Wilhelm would also place ducks, a cafe and a
drug dispensary in every one of the City's
eighty-two parks. Also, if called upon to serve,
he said he would spend his first week in City
Hall in the nude.

Free Street 23

"FREE BARTER
ON FREE (Haight) STREET SUNDAY.

WATCH FOR SIGNS
BRING YOUR STUFF
CLOTHES AND FABRICS
FOOD
KIDS' TOYS
FREE NEWS
ETC.

BRING DOWN WHAT YOU DON'T NEED
AND TAKE AWAY WHAT YOU WANT.
HAIGHT STREET WILL BE
FREE STREET SUNDAY.
CELEBRATE THE STREET.
CELEBRATE THE DAY.

CELEBRATE."

"A bunch of us went out back today and tore down the fence surrounding the yard. The neighbors, attracted by the sound of our laughter and shouting, gathered around to become infected with our delight and began to finger the claw hammers and crowbars which were scattered about. Suddenly one man leaped at his fence screaming "Cancer wood!" and that set it off.

"Before you knew it, all the fences in the block were down and all our neighbors were racing up and down the park they had built, congratulating each other for their boldness and imagination. We built a big fire to roast the turkey legs which Jon had brought over that morning. By mid-afternoon, people were fucking in the rosebushes, children were marauding in the turnip patch, and visionary conversations were going on in every corner of the garden. It was a hell of a day."

From a handbill distributed anonymously on Haight Street.

Sunday on Haight Street meant traffic snarls and crowds of weekend hippies and tourists.

Mime Troupe 🍳

The San Francisco Mime Troupe was the creation of Ronald Davis. He had worked previously as an assistant director with the Actors Workshop under Julius Irving and Herbert Blau. The Mime Troupe grew out of mime sessions; Davis gave mime lessons, and the Mime Troupe began with his enthusiastic students. During the formative days, Davis worked and lived in an old Baptist Church on Capp Street in the Mission district. Bill Ham, before he was a light show artist, was invited out to Capp Street to observe rehearsals for Sunday night productions at the church. Donations were taken at the door to see unstructured productions consisting mainly of dancers and musicians. People sat around on the floor with flutes and drums and trombones. A photographer projected a series of hand-colored slides. The effect of colored slides projected onto a group of free-form dancers added to a general freakiness. The spectacle fired the imagination.

John Conway of the San Francisco Park Commission, commenting on the Mime Troupe, said: "The Mime Troupe is out to undermine our society." "Yes, we are!" retorted Ron Davis. "The society that is hypocritical, that is imperialistic, that supports sham art, that supports sham wars, that censors dialogue, that has the crude audacity to call the opposition 'nervous Nellies,' must be undermined."

Emmett Grogan in the Mime Troupe Gorilla Band harbored a secret ambition to be an actor.

The San Francisco Mime Troupe was the creation of Ron Davis. They performed frequently in the Panhandle and other San Francisco public areas.

Mime Troupers without costumes substituted signs to identify their open theater roles.

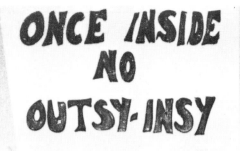

The Fillmore 23

Bill Graham

The rock music explosion in America was sparked by San Francisco musicians, and the Fillmore Auditorium was the showcase from which the entire rock music scene began. Bill Graham provided San Francisco with six years of weekend concerts. Two hundred and ninety-seven dates. It was a continous music festival, featuring the best rock and blues performers in the business. There were African dancers; a play, "The Beard," by Michael McClure; a wedding; even Lenny Bruce worked a gig at the Fillmore.

Early on, the police came down hard on Graham for promoting what the cops considered a bad influence on young people. But approving stories about the Fillmore in the *Chronicle* turned the tide, and the atmosphere at the ballroom was found to please everyone. The Flower Children of the Hashbury in their sometimes outrageous street clothes partied right alongside straight folks wearing sports jackets and ties and sunglasses. It was always an odd mix of people.

Until Graham opened the Fillmore with The Jefferson Airplane for Appeal II on December 10, 1965, the music scene in San Francisco was little more than a few jazz clubs with no dancing.

Graham's hard-driving formula for success set a new standard for the music industry. For a rock musician, a gig at the Fillmore was in itself important publicity, if not a crucial station to reach for success in the music business. The Jefferson Airplane, Grace Slick, Janis Joplin and Big Brother and the Holding Company, and The Grateful Dead played at Graham's concerts frequently. Between the venue served by the Fillmore and the Avalon, they became household names to their local and national fans.

Auditions for the Fillmore were held on Tuesday nights, and the price for admission was one dollar a head. The general freakiness level was a bit higher those nights, too. But Graham would not tolerate any "foolin' around." All the patrons had to maintain a level of decorum on the premises. Hell's Angels were not allowed wearing their colors, and no drugs could be used anywhere near Graham. All the same, stories abound about the acid trips that began there on the dance floor, in the middle of the strobes and liquid lights and the rolling bounding rhythms. One entered the Fillmore Auditorium from Geary Street, ascending a flight of stairs to a ticket hut, then left up some more steps to the second floor landing and the ballroom. Graham had a tiny office over the stairway next to a large coat checkroom.

Graham was in perpetual motion. He moved around his place with a purpose that seldom stopped. Clipboard in hand, Graham darted around on seemingly continuous errands. The feeling inside the Fillmore was one of controlled rock energy that flowed out of the darkened ballroom's interior, just off the entry hall which was decorated with posters and coming attraction announcements.

On either side of the entry to the dance floor, Graham set up tables that supported a continuous supply of penny candy, hard candy, suckers or apples, all free for the taking. On the last night of a featured performance, Graham and his crew gave away posters, too, adding fuel to the growing poster collecting craze.

Second floor lobby of Bill Graham's Fillmore Auditorium.

Bill Graham presents . . .

*Grace Slick, the singer with the
Jefferson Airplane, sat in Bill Graham's
office between sets at the Fillmore Auditorium.*

As Graham's enterprise accelerated, he worked in two time zones of consciousness, east coast time and west coast time—three hours apart. To aid him, he wore two wristwatches on his right arm to avoid confusion, that is, he wore two watches until his Swiss handmade Movado with two clock faces arrived from Geneva.

Graham's interest had once included acting, which he tried for a time during earlier days. The Fillmore provided an opportunity to develop his show business interests. His strengths lay in recognizing talent for his productions, and the energy to advance through the shark-infested waters of big-buck music kings who jealously guarded their domains. But while his competitors dropped out, Graham charged ahead with a singleness of purpose: money and the satisfaction of being the best in the business.

Strobe dancing in the Fillmore.

Janis Joplin

Grace Slick with Janis Joplin.

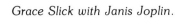

The Jefferson Airplane

The Fillmore Wedding.
The wedding ceremony was per-
formed for Lee Quanstrum and
Space Daisy who had asked
Graham if they could get married in
the Fillmore. Graham provided the
auditorium, champagne, and a
three-tier wedding cake as a gift.

Winterland 23

The Fillmore was a large dance hall, but during holidays and special occasions Graham moved his show over to an even larger auditorium in the Fillmore district — Winterland. It could accommodate ice shows or the circus.

Graham's biggest extravaganza of the year was the New Year's Eve party staged there. The midnight tolling included all the cheering and bands playing and the balloons, but when a loincloth-costumed figure emerged from the crowd freeing white doves while riding from the back of a white steed, the audience roared.

Poets and Posters 23

Allen Meyerson, director of The Committee.

Michael McClure was a beatnik-hippie. He was one of the youngest poets in San Francisco during the North Beach "beatnik" days of the 'fifties. His first public poetry reading was in 1955; at age 15 Michael McClure read alongside Allen Ginsberg, Gary Snyder, Lawrence Ferlinghetti and Kenneth Rexroth at the Six Gallery. He moved from North Beach to the Haight in 1962.

On July 24, 1966 Bill Graham put on a production of McClure's play "The Beard" at the Fillmore Auditorium. The play had been seen before on the east coast, and during a one-time presentation by the Actors Workshop at the Encore Theater. On the east coast, the play had received acclaim and accolades (two Obie awards). McClure's books of poetry had been published by Grove Press, City Lights and New Directions. His spectrum of friends included Hell's Angels in San Francisco, and Andy Warhol and company in New York, who had made a film of "The Beard."

Bill Graham's production of "The Beard" at the Fillmore was well-received, but some of the critics considered it "obscene." The play is a dialogue between Billy the Kid and Jean Harlow and consists of abusive, scolding remarks that develop and become a love ritual which ends with Billy going down on Jean at the fadeout.

The police told Graham that if he had one more performance of the "obscene" play, his dance hall permit would be taken away, so McClure took "The Beard" over to Alan Meyerson's Committee Theater in North Beach.

There the play was busted at the end of its first performance. The charge: Violation of Section 182, Suspicion of Conspiracy to Commit a Felony. In 1966 such an obvious sexual suggestion on stage in the public view was simply too much for those in

charge of public morals to bear. Yet down the street from the Committee Theater at a corner bar called the Garden of Eden, SRO audiences watched a nude couple acting out the real McCoy on stage, every hour on the hour. On the opposite corner, "topless" dancing was a big tourist attraction. But to arouse a sit-down cabaret theater crowd was something else. A saloon could present such a spectacle, but not a theater.

Ironically, Lenny Bruce had died in Los Angeles that same week at age 40, having devoted his career to exposing similar hypocrisy.

Lenny Bruce gave one of his great performances before a Fillmore audience. The hippies could relate to the Lenny Bruce passion of social satire.

Poster artists pose on the back steps of the Avalon Ballroom: (front row, right to left) Mouse, George Hunter, Bob Simon, Bob Fried, Rick Griffin, (back row, left to right) Satty, an Avalon guard, Victor Moscoso, Wes Wilson, and Alton Kelley.

Several days after the episode at the Committee Theatre, the San Francisco *Chronicle* printed a front-page story reporting another corruption of the public morals. This time the nastiness had been perpetrated with evil words—"dirty words." To make matters worse, the words had been printed under the guise of art—"dirty poetry." The hippies were at it again!

The outrage was a five-page booklet of poems by Lenore Kandel, "The Love Book." Lenore was characterized by the *Chronicle* as a "San Francisco housewife." She had also contributed her talents to the Diggers. Her "Love Book" was the talk of the town. "It's hard core pornography," said the cops. "Obscene," intoned inspector Peter Maloney of the Juvenile Bureau as he bought a copy for evidence at the Psychedelic Shop. Then he arrested the clerk of the store, who happened to be Allen Cohen. Cohen was helping out while Ron Thelin was away on business. The charge against Cohen was one of violating the California anti-obscenity code. He was arrested and then booked at Park Station.

A crowd grew around the Psychedelic Shop. Some of the hippies ran across the street to the *Oracle* office above the Print Mint and made up some picket signs for a protest. The signs read: "Burn all Books" and "Ban the Bible." To add to the revelry Lenore Kandel drove up to the scene in a cab. "Is it true that my book has been busted? Far out!"

A week later Allen Cohen and Ron Thelin appeared at City Hall. At the court arraignment Ron was arrested as the owner of the Psychedelic Shop. He was responsible for selling items that could "excite vicious or lewd thoughts or acts." The cover illustration on the book of poems was recognized as more "obscene art!" Another outrage. The cover depicts a buddha "coupled with a voluptuous maiden."

The poems in "The Love Book" are essentially expressions of ecstasy that make no distinction between the ecstasy of lovemaking and the ecstasy of religion.

"It's blasphemy," said one judge, and the District Attorney forbade his wife ever to read "The Love Book."

Out at San Francisco State College, several teachers announced a "civic cultural program" as part of the college's Poetry Center. The teachers would offer themselves to commit "acts of academic defiance . . . to protest against harassment and censorship of the arts." "The Love Book," they said, "is a sincere effort and should be judged on that ground." Three professors of English got themselves arrested for reading "The Love Book" and Michael McClure's "The Beard" in the San Francisco State campus bookstore. The little book of poems very soon became a Bay area collector's item.

In the weeks and months that followed, both "The Love Book" and Michael McClure's play "The Beard" were used as test cases illustrating what proponents considered to be the growing cancer in the arts and literature, but cooler heads prevailed. The First Amendment of the Constitution solved the matter when the California State Supreme Court ultimately reviewed the case and reversed the decision of the lower courts.

Satty. The artist as an object in his art. Satty externalized the energy of rock music and the frenzied action going on in the ballrooms and in the parks. His work was a harmonic, often created while the printing press was in motion. Satty began by printing impression, then overprinting, sometimes overprinting several times to achieve a desired result. Many of his posters became one of a kind, unique prints that emerged after lengthy sessions on a two-color press at Hal Kramer's Orbit Graphic Arts.

The San Francisco poster renaissance was sparked in the Haight-Ashbury beginning with the success of a poster by Lorin Gillette during the summer of '65, the "love" poster. It was a 17" x 23" vertical format black and white photographic reproduction of a couple embracing on Ocean Beach. Floating above them is printed the word "love." Gillette distributed his poster to shops around the city from his store on Divisadero Street next to The Magic Theater For Mad Men Only.

Around the corner, at 1090 Page Street, Chet Helms used posters to advertise the final weeks of his 50-cent jam sessions in the "ballroom." One of Chet's poster artists was Alton Kelley; Kelley knew George Hunter and became one of the decorators of the saloon in Virginia City. Kelley created the Red Dog's front-of-the-store sign, a large wooden circle painted red with a design of the RCA Victor dog.

There was a Red Dog Saloon poster featuring the Charlatans, which might well be the first psychedelic rock 'n 'roll advertisement. It had the look of a western sheriff's "Wanted" poster. George Hunter's interest in Maxfield Parrish also emerged out of those early dance advertisements. The western '49er style had a decided influence on the hippie character and fashion in the years to come.

The dance posters were basically distributed as advertisements, getting the word to the public about the coming attractions. Within a short time, social commentary became a subject of posters, too. Posters first appeared on telephone poles and later in store windows. Late in '65 and early in '66, Bill Graham drove to Bay area colleges, up and down Telegraph Avenue in Berkeley, and on Haight Street, stapling his dance posters wherever he could find a good space.

By the summer of 1966, Graham's posters began to be recognized as art. He quickly realized that as soon as posters were stapled to telephone poles they were removed by a growing poster-collecting public.

Posters were given away free on the final night of each week's show at the Fillmore. By 1968, San Francisco dance poster art was receiving worldwide attention. During 1969 the Museum of Modern Art in New York put on an extended exhibition of dance poster art that included the work of Wes Wilson, Bonnie Graham, Stanley Mouse, Lee Conklin, Randy Tuten, David Singer, David Byrd, and Victor Moscoso.

There was a family feeling about the Haight-Ashbury. Outrageous but civilized conduct and tribal costumes were accepted and even expected. Downtown such behavior was a sure way to attract negative attention. Long hair and beads were

equated with hippie custom as were drugs. It was all show. A surreal spectacle. A psychedelic circus with bands and dancing and people all dressed up having a good time. In many ways Ken Kesey was at the head of the circus. And his bus, the 1939 International Harvester, loaded with Merry Pranksters, led the whole thing down the road.

San Francisco was the free-swinging place to be during the winter of '65. Magic music was in the air, and a growing number of people responded to its rhythm. Ken Kesey's odyssey was skipping along in his 1939 International Harvester bus. The psychedelic bus had returned to its La Honda retreat. But Kesey's lifestyle was under increasing public scrutiny; Gerd Stern had cast off from Gate 5 in Sausalito with his nurse and Steve Durkee to explore new time zones with USCO; Stewart Brand was seeking the original American Indian; Ramon Sendor was composing tape language; Ben Jacopetti had reinvented open theater; Alan Myerson had opened the Committee; Joan Baez had started the Free University; rock bands were forming; and Jerry Mander was saving the Grand Canyon from becoming a dam.

The Trips Festival 23

Stewart Brand
The Whole Earth Man

In January 1966, Jerry Mander, an associate of ad man Howard Gossage, held a meeting at his office in North Beach; it was a cosmic clutch— Jerry, Stewart Brand, Ramon Sendor and Ben Jacopetti. They had come together to discuss a program of fun and games soon to be unleashed on the general public. Until that meeting, the so-called underground action had been a few "benefits" and "Acid Tests" with limited gates. The audience had been made up of friends, friends of friends, and a few deserving worthies from U.C. Berkeley and S.F. State.

Kesey was at the head of a circus. A literary cult star, his first novel, *One Flew Over the Cuckoo's Nest,* made Kesey a personality for the press to follow. Ken's bohemian behavior was observed and recorded with growing interest. More so than some of the other craziness that was going on around town, Kesey's *cannabis* arrests had also made front page news.

One morning in the fall of '65, prankster Mike Keegan, in the merry band of Kesey's circus makers, was at the door of Stewart Brand's North Beach apartment on Vallejo Street. Keegan had dropped in to tell Stewart about a Stinson Beach "Acid Test." One of a series of events that the "Captain," Ken Kesey, had been holding around the Bay area. This latest event had not come off too well, said Keegan. It wasn't "together." Events should be indoors for better control, he told Stewart. The decibel range was important. But people were responding in some far out ways. Stewart Brand could relate to that. Stewart was a photographer and a visionary. He could see the new wave coming. That got Stewart to cogitating and considering.

The time had arrived for consolidation, to stop and develop the new planes of consciousness that were emerging around the Bay area. There were a lot of people making some interesting discoveries, but the domains of these energies were widely separated. No one really knew how many people "out there" wanted to be turned on, but things were changing. The success of Bill Graham's Appeal I and Appeal II had helped prove that. Kesey's "Acid Tests" were getting revered whispers; so had Chet Helms' 1090 jam sessions and his California Hall dance; Bill Ham's Pine Street "lights" had been noted, and several local rock groups were gaining in popularity. A new day was dawning.

There was a need to celebrate the new feelings, the higher consciousness that people were trying to express. The time had come to commemorate all the good trips with a "Trips Festival."

The meeting at Jerry Mander's office was called by Stewart Brand. Stewart had been amazed at the amount of work he could accomplish just by picking up the telephone. He had talked with Kesey and others about joining together for a big public event. Mander would help with the promotion. There was no real model for the program that Stewart had in mind. There were no agents or promoters or places that could work within the framework of the programs that he wanted. It was an all-new form of show biz.

Participation seemed to be the key word for it all. Audience participation had been a traditional element for success. If the audience would participate as they did in the benefits and at the Kesey "Acid Tests," then everyone would come and have a good time. Everyone would be on his or her own trip.

The relative smoothness and super energy that Bill Graham had displayed managing the Mime Troupe benefits had been noted by many people. The programs had been a success. So Graham was called in by Jerry Mander to work out the ticket problems and general management for the expected crowd at the Trips Festival. Graham responded with one of his frequent displays of energy and enthusiasm. He would manage the Trips Festival "for free," he said, just for the opportunity, just for the fun of it, and for his own personal celebration.

The Longshoremen's Hall on Beach Street near Fisherman's Wharf was available for $1200 a weekend. The octagonal building was new and it was big. Three thousand people could fit inside; that would make a good crowd.

"The general tone of things has moved on from the self-conscious happenings to a more jubilant occasion where the audience participates because it's more fun to do so than not. Audience dancing is an assumed part of all the shows, and the audience is invited to wear ecstatic dress and to bring their own gadgets (A.C. outlets will be provided)."

"Electronic Performance!
A new medium of
communication & entertainment
A drugless PSYCHEDELIC experience.
Presenting:
The Ken Kesey Merry Band of Pranksters
and
The Psychedelic Symphony,

Ben Jacopetti
and
selections from the Open Theatre
including
the Jazz Mice
Beatle Readings
the Endless Explosion
the God Box
the Congress of Wonders and other wonders

Stewart Brand's
"America Needs Indians,
Parades and Changes;"

Big Brother and the Holding Company

the Grateful Dead

Ron Boise and the
Electric Thunder sculpture

Hell's Angels

Allen Ginsberg

the Dancers Workshop

Vortex

Marshall MacLuhan

Neal Cassidy vs Ann Murphy Vaudeville

the Stroboscopic Trampoline

and you,
whatever it is."

Press Release for the Trips Festival issued by Jerry Mander

"An LSD experience without LSD"—that was a laugh. In fact, the heads are pouring in by the hundreds, bombed out of their gourds, hundreds of heads coming out into the absolute open for the first time. It is like the time the Pranksters went to the Beatles concert in full costume, looking so bizarre and so totally *smashed* that no one could believe they were. Nobody would *risk* it in public like this. Well, the kids are just having an LSD experience without LSD, that's all, and this is what it looks like. A hulking crazed whirlpool. That's nice. Lights and movies sweeping around the hall; five movie projectors going and God knows how many light machines, interferrometrics, the intergalactic science-fiction seas all over the walls, loudspeakers studding the hall all the way around like flaming chandeliers, strobes exploding, black lights with Day-Glo objects under them and Day-Glo paint to play with, street lights at every entrance flashing red and yellow, two bands, the Grateful Dead and Big Brother and the Holding Company and a troop of weird girls in leotards leaping around the edges blowing dog whistles—and the Pranksters. Paul Foster has wrapped black friction tape all around his shoes and up over his ankles and swaddled his legs and hips and torso in it up to his rib cage, where begins a

white shirt and then white bandaging all over his face and skull and just a slit for his eyes, over which he wears dark glasses. He also wears a crutch and a sign saying, "You're in the Pepsi Generation and I'm a pimply freak!" Rotor! Also heads from all over, in serapes and mandala beads and Indian headbands and Indian beads, the great era for all that, and one in a leather jerkin with "Under Ass Wizard Mojo Indian fighter" stenciled on the back. Mojo! Oh the freaking strobes turning every brain stem into a cauliflower erupting into corrugated ping-pong balls—*can't stand it* — and a girl rips off her shirt and dances bare-breasted with her great mihs breaking up into an endless stream of ruby-red erect nipples streaming out of the great milk-and-honey under the strobe lights. The dancing is ecstatic, a nice macaroni of braless breasts jiggling and cupcake bottoms wiggling and multiple arms writhing and leaping about. Thousands of straight intellectuals and culturati and square hippies, North Beach style, gawking and learning. Dr. Francis Rigney, psychiatrist to the Beat Generation, looking on, and all the Big Daddies left over from the Beat period, Eric "Big Daddy" Nord and Tom "Big Daddy" Donahue, and the press, vibrating under Ron Boise's thunder machine. A great rout in progress, you understand."

Excerpted from *The Electric Kool-aid Acid Test* by Tom Wolfe

The first night of the Trips Festival was madness personified. For Bill Graham, "nothing seemed to be going right. The lights were wrong, the wiring strung out all over the place was illegal, speakers were out. It was an insurance man's headache and a fire marshal's nightmare. There were problems in the ticket booth. Chaos seemed to reign.

"Then just before the auditorium doors were opened to the public, I looked across the hall to the opposite exit doors. There is this person, this somebody in a silver spacesuit with a space helmet, holding open the exit doors to let people into the hall. Just ushering people into this circus that I'd been trying to organize for the past four days. So I rushed through the hall to the exits yelling 'What the fuck is going on? What the hell are you doing?' At the exit doors this spacesuited person flips up the face guard and I recognize the guy who was at the Fillmore for the Acid Test. He yells back, 'Hi, it's me, it's all right. These are just a few of my friends.' Well, it sure as hell wasn't OK with me. I didn't care who this guy was. I was responsible for putting on a show and I damned well didn't want anyone ruining everything I had worked so hard to do. So I screamed and yelled and carried on. Everytime spaceman tried to explain, I just cut him off by pouring out more of my anger. Then at the peak of my madness, when I'm ready to boil over, ready to burst, screaming, 'So do you know what I mean? Do you damned well know what I'm saying?' Space Captain flipped the lid of his space helmet shut and walked away. At first I was stunned. I couldn't believe it. People don't do that. Then I began to laugh. My temper was broken. It made me feel good. The spaceman was Ken Kesey. That was the first time we met."

With the Trips Festival all things rock 'n 'roll started to change. Until the beginning of the new year, 1966, the bands had not considered themselves professional musicians, at least not enough to have joined a union. The only musicians who had joined the San Francisco Musicians' Union had been jazz people who played with touring bands or in the jazz clubs. The Family Dog was getting some hints from the union, and so were the Charlatans. But the Trips Festival affected the whole underground art movement in San Francisco. No one had made any money from most of the parties. Unless a profit was made, the unions, up to that time, generally let people alone. That was underground art, and the underground artist supported his habit in the traditional mode, working in music shops and giving music lessons on the side. A few artists received some funding from grants. The GI Bill was keeping others afloat, and driving a cab was fun for awhile. The first band to have a real gig, with a real contract was the Jefferson Airplane.

The Trips Festival symbolized a wedding ceremony between the underground artists and the public, between the press, the city fathers, and the people. It was a psychedelic spectacle that was all new to the straight world. It was a shocker, but a fun trip to contemplate. Official San Francisco was also adequately signaled that a new wave was on its way. Some fireworks were ignited too.

The three-day weekend at the Longshoremen's Hall included just about every sight and sound trip available. Kesey's "Psychedelic Symphony" played with the Grateful Dead to a light show created by a sound-light console set on a tower in the middle of the hall. Films and overhead projections and 50 flashlights danced over the walls. Neal Cassidy dressed as a gorilla, chased Ann Murphy.

Stroboscopic Trampoline, Allen Ginsberg, and Hell's Angels entertained with the "Pin Ball Machine" and the "Endless Explosion, the God Box," the "Congress of Wonders" and more wonders till the weekend came to an end.

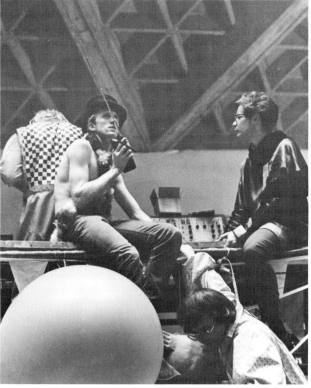

During the weekend of the Trips Festival and the previous weekend, the Tape Music Center out on Divisadero Street put on a program of improvised music with a light show. The production was called "Vision in Motion" and billed as "spontaneous light and sound compositions." The lights were the work of Bill Ham and Tony Martin.

Herb Caen. When his column in the San Francisco Chronicle *mentioned the success of the Trips Festival the item sparked some fireworks and changes that affected the whole rock scene.*

Two days after the Trips Festival, Jerry Mander mentioned to Herb Caen during a Banducci soiree at Enrico's Coffee House that the Trips Festival weekend at the Longshoremen's Hall had been a smashing success. It had made a good profit. A sixteen-thousand-dollar profit!

It also made a good story for Herb Caen's column in the *Chronicle*. The item appeared the next morning. A phone call from the San Francisco Musicians' Union to the Longshoremen's Union came soon after. Was it true that one of the heaviest unions in the country had just let a bunch of scabs run a profit-making enterprise inside their own mother-loving headquarters? Had the longshoremen really let non-union musicians play a sold-out concert inside their hiring hall? Hell's teeth, that had to be some kind of historical first.

The Summer Solstice ☯

The summer solstice is the one day of the year when the sun is at its highest: And of course such a ritual day was not forgotten by the hippies who trooped up to Twin Peaks, the hills behind the Hashbury, to welcome the sun from that highest point of the city. The crowd of flower folk gathered before dawn. They camped out on the eastern side of the grassy slopes to welcome that good day sunshine with chants and drums, incense and bells and flags, while the first rays of the sun flited through a morning fog. Amid a soaring sky rocket and red and white flares, Charlie Brown stood up and proclaimed the beginning of the Summer of Love.

Summer solstice celebrants descending from Twin Peaks above the Hashbury (preceding page).

Love Pageant Rally

Sam

In September 1966, 1090 Page was busted. On the night of the bust someone had sailed a coke bottle out of one of the third floor windows. Unfortunately the missile fell at the feet of a couple of strolling cops. The reaction from the police was to arrest someone. But it was an illegal bust, said the tenants.

The bust at 1090 caused a stir that erupted into a sign-carrying demonstration of several dozen angry people. The coke bottle in question had unfortunately landed at the feet of a couple of police-men, and their reaction was to arrest someone. It was an illegal bust, said the tenants. The demonstrators decided to parade down Haight Street to Park Station in protest.

On Thursday morning at approximately 2:05 A.M. four uniformed officers of the SFPD entered the back door at 1090 Page. The officers entered after a coke bottle was thrown out of a third floor window. The officers checked the ID's of the occupants of the room. A young man, Vince Dalviso, was appre-hended and forced to open his room clothes closet where certain illegal drugs were found. Mr. Dalviso was removed to a patrol car and taken to Park Station and booked for posses-sion of marijuana, a violation of P.C. 11530. A charge with a maximum penalty of ten years in prison.

From a handbill distributed anonymously on Haight Street.

The parade of protesters marched past the Drugstore Cafe at the corner of Masonic and Haight. Inside, having a coffee at a window seat and watch-ing the demonstration zig-zag its way through the traffic, was the original psychedelic ranger, Michael Bowen, with his friend Allen Cohen. "You know," said Allen, looking at the angry faces and the signs reading *Illegal Bust* and *Police Are Paid to Protect Us from What?* There should be some way to stop all this negative energy. If people aren't demonstrating against civil rights violations, it's the war in Vietnam. We should be able to turn some of this bad energy into something more positive." "Yeah," replied Michael, "and the way to do it is with a show of elbow-to-elbow crowds displaying a unified protest against unjust political acts."

Michael and Allen continued drinking their coffee and staring after the retreating demonstrators. It was at that point that they conceived the idea for a Panhandle event, the Love Pageant Rally. That event created the energy that produced the Human Be-In. It would be a coming together of the tribes. A gathering of tens of thousands of people.

On October 6, 1966, California outlawed the use of LSD. To most observers the date had little significance, but to others who were affected by the moratorium, the date took on a mystical meaning. October 6, 1966, was equated with "666." The symbol "666" is found in Revelation in the Bible, the Cabala, the Masonic, and other mystical orders. It stands for "the Beast." All names for the Antichrist have 666 as their numerical equivalent. A Greek symbol that signified the demonic, the lower mind, has as its numerical equivalent 666. In the Bible, Revelation 13:18, the Beast was the Roman Empire.

The emergence of the Beast was at hand once again, thought Michael Bowen. LSD had been their right. "Why was it taken away?" he asked. "A democracy is the people telling their government what makes them happy, not the other way around." The road to Eleusis was proving to have more obstacles than had been thought.

Instead of protesting the lack of communication between the police and the street people, and the moratorium of LSD, Bowen and Cohen considered alternate ways to bring attention to the growing problems that existed in the Haight-Ashbury. The pri-

mary problem was communication—communication between official San Francisco and the growing numbers of Hashbury hippies. The traditional modes of protest were not working; they were too confrontational and produced accelerating action and reaction.

The synchronistic aspects of October 6, 1966, suggested to Bowen and Cohen a worthwhile date to take advantage of. "Instead of protesting the moratorium of LSD," said Cohen, "instead of protesting the law that was going into effect, our idea was to make a demonstration which would show the law's falsity. Without confrontation. We wanted to create a celebration of innocence. We were not guilty of using illegal substances. We were celebrating transcendental consciousness. The beauty of the universe. The beauty of being."

"Bring the color Gold,
    bring photos of personal saints and gurus
        and heroes of the underground . . .
            bring children . . . flowers . . . flutes . . .
                drums . . . feathers . . . bands . . . beads . . .
                    banners, flags, incense, chimes, gongs,
                        cymbals, . . . symbols, costumes and JOY."

Permissions for a Love Pageant Rally were requested and invitations sent out to Mayor Shelley, Assemblyman Willie Brown, Federal Attorney Cecil Poole, Chief of Police Tom Cahill, and whoever else Bowen and Cohen could think of at the time. October 6 was only ten days away.

> *To whom it may concern:*
>
> *We are planning a Love Pageant Rally on October 6, 1966, at 2 P.M. at Panhandle Park between Masonic Avenue and Ashbury Street as described in the enclosed announcement.*
>
> *We would like a permit for our gathering. There will be no food or wares sold. Our party will be a celebration of community awareness and joy in communion with an international fellowship of those interested in the exploration of consciousness.*
>
> *Your advice would be appreciated. Thank you.*
>
> *Sincerely yours,*
>
> *Citizens for a Love Pageant Rally of October 6, 1966.*

The letter to the Parks and Recreation Department.

Sir:

Opposition to an unjust law creates futility for citizens who are its victims and increases the hostility between the governed and the governors. In the case of the LSD prohibition, the State has entered directly into the sacrosanct, personal psyches of its citizens. Our Love Pageant Rally is intended to overcome the paranoia and separation with which the State wishes to divide and silence the increasing revolutionary sense of Californians. Similar rallies will be held in communities such as ours all over the country and in Europe. You are invited to attend and address our rally. Thank you.

Sincerely yours,

Citizens for the Love Pageant Rally of October 6, 1966.

The Love Pageant Rally invitation which was dispatched to Mayor John F. Shelley and city officials gave a hint of Psychedelic Ranger philosophy.

Berkeley Barb
publisher
Max Scheer

The Grateful Dead.

A declaration of personal freedom
was drawn up by the Psychedelic Rangers:

A Prophecy of A Declaration of Independence

When in the flow of human events it becomes necessary for the people to cease to recognize the obsolete
social patterns which have isolated man from his consciousness and to create with the youthful energies of
the world revolutionary communities of harmonious relations to which the two-billion-year-old life process en-
titles them, a decent respect to the opinions of mankind
should declare the causes which impel them to this creation. We hold these experiences to be self-evident,
that all is equal, that the creation endows us with certain
inalienable rights, that among these are: The freedom
of body, the pursuit of joy, and the expansion of consciousness, and that to secure these rights, we the citizens of the earth declare our love and compassion for
all conflicting hate-carrying men and women of the
world. We declare the identity of flesh and consciousness; all reason and law must respect and protect this
holy identity.

The first translation of this prophecy into political
action will take place October 6, 1966. (666 . . . the
mark of the ascension of the beast.)

The date that the California law prohibiting the pos-
session of LSD comes into effect, the day of the fear-
produced legislation against the expansion of consciousness. At 2 P.M. in the PANHANDLE at MASONIC and
OAK we will gather IN A LOVE PAGEANT
RALLY . . . to affirm our identity, community, and innocence from influence of the fear addiction of the general public as symbolized in this law. Copies of the
prophecy of our Declaration of Independence, living
morning glory plants and mushrooms will be presented
at 2 P.M. to San Francisco Mayor Shelley at City Hall;
Cecil Poole, U.S. Attorney General for Northern
California, at the Federal Building; and Captain Kiely of
the S.F. Police Department. Similar demonstrations will
be held at the same time in New York, Los Angeles,
London and Amsterdam.

The first week of October 1966 was heavy. The moon was full. The Beast was on the prowl. The Beast's coming was heralded in the streets; the Fillmore and Hunter's Point districts were in turmoil. A young man had been shot and killed for purportedly stealing an automobile at Hunter's Point. The incident touched off a four-day riot. Street fires, gunshots in the night, and Molotov cocktails rocked the city.

But while the fires were burning and the sirens were screaming, Winterland, in the heart of the Fillmore district, was cooking. Jefferson Airplane, Butterfield Blues Band, and Muddy Waters. With afternoon concerts, too. Out in the Haight, Cohen and staff were preparing the third issue of the *Oracle*. Letters were sent out to various city departments and local politicos reminding them of the Love Pageant Rally from the *Oracle* office. To be on the staff of the *Oracle* was strictly voluntary. But everyone worked hard and everything was accomplished in time. The third San Francisco *Oracle* got to press and the Love Pageant Rally became reality.

"Ugh!"

On Thursday morning, the sixth, the staff of the
Oracle and the Psychedelic Shop employees
became the delegation for the Love Pageant Rally.
They converged on City Hall in full golden-hued
costume bearing morning glory seeds, flowers, and
store-bought mushrooms (symbolizing psychedelic
mushrooms) in order to "turn on" Mayor Shelley.
The press turned out for the show—the hippies were
always good for a giggle.

The press missed the point of the Love Pageant Rally delegation, and anyway the big counter-culture story for that day had been covered in the morning *Chronicle*. The paper had printed a headline story about Ken Kesey, who was, at that point, a fugitive from the law. There had been a misunderstanding involving less than an ounce of pot. Then Kesey had fled to Mexico, but had sneaked back into San Francisco for a secret meeting, an "exclusive interview" with Donovan Bess of the *Chronicle*. Earlier in the week, Bess revealed, Kesey had participated in a "Super Trips Festival" out at San Francisco State. Also on the previous day Kesey had talked with students at Stanford University during an English class about creativity. Kesey had also returned, he said, as a gesture of defiance to the FBI, "To put some salt in the wounds of J. Edgar Hoover."

Poet Michael McClure took French film director Christian Marquand to the Love Pageant Rally. Marquand was casting a new film, *Candy*, and was in San Francisco looking for a young girl to play the ingenue. Marquand asked McClure if he would aid him in his search for "an attractive youth of the hippie generation." Michael suggested the 666 event. There would be acres of blossoming flower children, he said. The film director liked the idea, so McClure and Marquand drove out to the Haight in a long, black, chauffeured limousine. At the Panhandle they walked among Sherwood Forest cum Salvation Army, straight and free-swinging multitudes, until Marquand spotted his prize. She was everything he was looking for. This would be his new star. "This is it," he said, "this is she." He walked up to the lucky damsel. The first words out of Marquand's mouth were, "Hi! Would you like to be in the movies?"

The lovely, almond-eyed flower child turned and looked Marquand straight in the eye. She regarded him as if he were a wet garden slug. "Fuck you, Buster," she said then faded back into the crowd.

The Love Pageant Rally was a smashing success. Michael Bowen and Allen Cohen stood on the broad path that led into the Panhandle from Oak and Clayton Streets and discussed their achievement. The paths and open spaces were jammed with people. A newly painted red flatbed truck was set up as a stage for the Grateful Dead, Janis Joplin, and Big Brother and the Holding Company. Dick Alpert walked by and was hailed by Bowen. "Isn't it far out?" he said. "People are sure hungry for some communicating. They love it. It's a joyous moment. What do you think, Alpert?" Alpert agreed that the rally was indeed successful.

"We should do it again," suggested Allen Cohen.

"Yeah," replied Bowen. "But next time, I'll bet we could get ten times the people."

"What would you call this event, Alpert?" asked Cohen. "It's more than a rally."

"Well," said Alpert, "it's a hell of a gathering. It's just being. Humans being. Being together."

"Yeah," said Bowen. "It's a Human Be-In."

Marsha Thelin walked up to Allen and said, "We're not dismayed. Laws will change."

Well," said Bowen, "we'll just have another rally. Only bigger. And next time we bring all the tribes together."

Dancing in the Panhandle (next page).

That night Michael Bowen and Allen Cohen had a powwow. In the back of Michael's flat was a square room with a single small window, Michael's meditation room. Mattresses covered with Indian batiks lay on the floor. Entry to the room was made with respect. Shoes off. Incense and flowers sat on a low round table in the middle of the room. Triple-eyed Indians and vibrating Buddha figures stared down from the walls. Michael shook off his sandals and walked across the mattresses with a phone in his hand. He plugged the phone into a wall jack and dialed. "I've got to call my guru down in Mexico," he said, "and let him know how beautiful this day has been."

Michael Bowen called his spiritual adviser, John Cooke, in Cuernavaca, Mexico. Their conversation conceived the plan for the biggest event to be held in the Haight. The Human Be-In. The model Be-In.

The next night, Big Brother and the Holding Company, Jim Queskin's Jug Band, and the Electric Train held the fort at Chet Helm's Avalon Ballroom. At the Fillmore the program was the Butterfield Blues Band, the Jefferson Airplane, and the Grateful Dead. The Civic Auditorium featured the Mamas and the Papas, and the Association. All in all it was a *heavy* week.

Now Day 23

A street event, a party to "celebrate the rebirth of the Haight and the death of money now" was held on Haight Street. It was another guerrilla theater gala with the Mime Troupers and Diggers and party favors. The festivities began with white-sheeted nymphets handing out to the street people and tourists strips of paper that had been silk-screened with six-inch red letters. The strips read "Now." The nubiles also gave away penny whistles and flowers and fruit and incense sticks. The troops split up into groups on both sides of Haight Street between Ashbury and Clayton, chanting. One group started with "Ooooooooooh!" They were answered by the group on the opposite side of the street who echoed with "Aaaaaaaaah!" Then the first group cried out in louder voice: "Ssssssssssh!" And the other side of the street answered, "Be cool!" "Ooooooooooh!" "Aaaaaaaaah!" "Ssssssssssh!" "Be cool!" They chanted in turn from each side of the Street. Someone distributed flutes. Others gave away oranges and bunches of grapes. The crowd on the street began to swell. Traffic slowed a bit. A Muni bus stopped. The driver climbed out, did a cake walk, then got back on the bus and drove away to wild applause. The sidewalk was elbow-to-elbow crowds spilling into the street. Another chant was taken up: "The streets belong to the people! The streets belong to the people!" The kids went crazy with whistles and chants. It was a good party.

But the cops didn't think so. They drove up in a paddy wagon. Two three-wheeled motorcycle cops zipped up and down the street admonishing the hippies to break it up and go home. The hippies yelled back, "The streets belong to the people!"

When the street was finally cleared and the traffic started to flow, "Hairy Henry" Kot, a Hell's Angel, drove down Haight Street popping and backfiring aboard his Harley-Davidson hog. Standing up, perched on the back waving a "NOW" banner, was Phyllis Willner, screaming with glee, "Freeeeeeee!"

The police didn't see anything to party about. On the contrary, they looked around for someone to account for all this tomfoolery—disturbing the peace and all that. Someone would indeed be busted. Phyllis and the driver of the motorcycle had committed a grievous breach of the traffic code. To wit: Phyllis had stood up on a moving vehicle. That violation was compounded by the fact that her driver happened to be a notorious Hell's Angel—Hairy Henry Kot. He had recently been released from San Quentin. Now he was a parole violator and in deep trouble, so the cops busted Kot on the spot.

Hairy Henry was in the company of a "brother," "Chocolate George" Hendricks. Chocolate George, true to the Hell's Angels battle code of "All on one, and one on all," responded in the only way he could, with a brief tirade. So Chocolate George was taken to the slammer for his efforts.

Gabe Katz, an Oracle artist, carried his dog, Man, during the street celebration.

The sidewalks quickly filled with people who stopped to see the show unfolding around them. Hippies and tourists all seemed to be taking part in a circus parade on Haight Street.

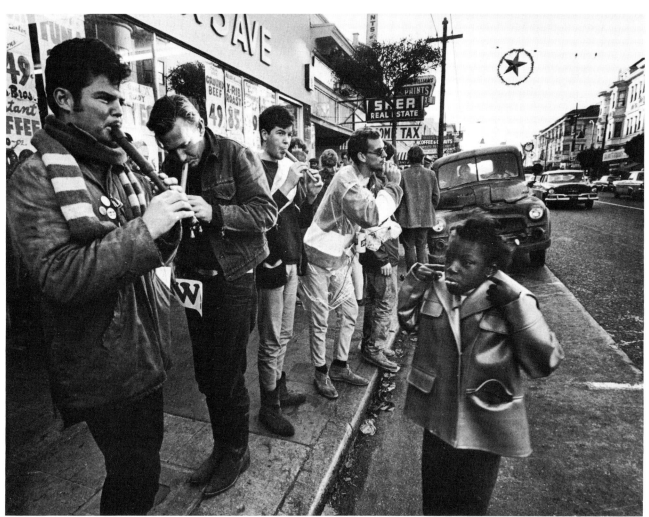

*It was a classic Digger street hap-
pening with puppet figures designed
by sculptor La Mortadella parading
down Haight Street with a coffin of
money to represent the "Death of
Money, Now."*

NOW!

Phyllis Willner stood on the back of
Hell's Angel Hairy Henry Kot's
chopped Harley-Davidson wailing
"Frrrrrrreeeeeeeeeeeeeee!"

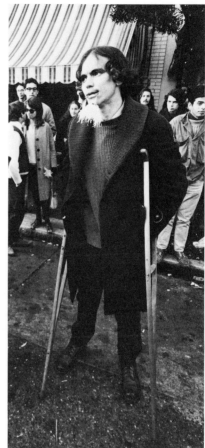

Phyllis was questioned by the police about her role in the traffic infringement that occurred on Haight Street with Hairy Henry. Hell's Angel Chocolate George looked on, standing in front of the Digger free store. The Free Frames of Reference lean against the building.

The traffic violation on Haight Street caused swift justice to prevail. Two police cars and a paddy wagon responded with a total of six cops.

Phyllis took the police inside the Free Store for a free look around. One cop admired an object. "Take it," said Phyllis, "it's yours." That got a good laugh all around.

Chocolate George was arrested and taken in the roundup, too.

The word spread fast up on Haight Street: Chocolate George and Hairy Henry had been busted. Chocolate George was a folk hero; he was more visual than most Angels, and his fondness for symbolic decoration endeared him to the rest of the symbol-wearing community. Now their man was in jail.

The crowd milling about on Haight Street was informed of the Angel bust and quickly formed ranks and started walking west. The Mime Troupe theatrics combined with the Diggers' energy to inspire a new chant: "Free the Angels!" "Free the Angels!" At the end of Haight Street, the marchers turned onto Stanyan Street and headed for Park Police Station at the edge of Golden Gate Park.

The crowd on Haight Street headed for Park Police Station in a party mood, chanting, "Free the Angels."

141

When a hundred marchers descended upon Park Station, they were met by police barring the door. The good-natured crowd started chanting, "Free Henry Kot! Free Chocolate George!" A black-draped coffin and masked pallbearers created a carnival atmosphere. A statement was sent out to the hippies from the desk sergeant: Bail would be set at $2,500. If ten percent of that amount could be raised, bail would be posted and the men would be set free. Immediately the marchers commenced an intensive pass-the-coffin campaign with another chant: "Angels in jail, money for bail." Everyone gave something. Even the police guarding the station house dipped into their pockets and added to the donations. The necessary amount was quickly collected and "Chocolate George" was released. Mr. Kot was detained a while longer.

The president of the San Francisco chapter of Hell's Angels, "Angel Pete," was overwhelmed by the generosity of the hippies. He said he would not forget them, and true to his word the San Francisco Hell's Angels reciprocated with a party in the Panhandle, "The New Year's Day Wail." The Angels provided beer, a flatbed truck, a PA system, and the Grateful Dead.

The police guarding the station were the first to contribute to the bail.

Michael McClure, Freewheelin' Frank, Richard Brautigan with the crowd confronted the cops at the station house.

The Human Be-In 🙐

T he building that housed
the Print Mint was a
deep store front with cherry
wood paneled office space in
back. The H.I.P. job co-op
started there (Haight Indepen-
dent Proprietors), and upstairs
was the original *Oracle* office
before it moved down the
street to Michael's place.

Jerry Rubin and Gary Snyder

The Print Mint sold all the popular posters of the
day. The foot traffic buying the latest posters got to
be heavy at times. Early in January, 1967, the media was invited to a press conference called by
Bowen and Cohen in back of the Print Mint.

PRESS RELEASE

January 12, 1967

*For ten years a new nation has grown inside the
robot flesh of the old. Before your eyes a new free vital
soul is reconnecting the living centers of the American
body.*

*On January 12, 1967, at 10 A.M. at 1542 Haight
Street, behind the Print Mint, Gary Snyder, Michael
Bowen, Jerry Rubin, Allen Cohen, Jay Thelin will en-
tertain the press and answer questions about the Gathering of the Tribes for a Human Be-In on January 14,
1967 at the Polo Fields in Golden Gate Park.*

*Berkeley political activists and the love generation of
the Haight-Ashbury will join together with members of
the new nation who will be coming from every state in
the nation, every tribe of the young (the emerging soul
of the nation) to powwow, celebrate, and prophesy the
epoch of liberation, love, peace, compassion and unity
of mankind. The night of bruited fear of the American
eagle-breast-body is over. Hang your fear at the door
and join the future. If you do not believe, please wipe
your eyes and see.*

Human Be-In poster by Michael Bowen.

Allen Cohen

A Gathering of the Tribes

A union of love and activism previously separated by categorical dogma and label mongering will finally occur ecstatically when Berkeley political activists and hip community and San Francisco's spiritual generation and contingents from the emerging revolutionary generation all over California meet for a Gathering of the Tribes for a Human Be-In at the Polo Fields in Golden Gate Park on Saturday, January 14, 1967, from 1 to 5 P.M.

Twenty to fifty thousand people are expected to gather for a joyful PowWow and Peace Dance to be celebrated with leaders, guides and heroes of our generation: Timothy Leary will make his first Bay Area public appearance; Allen Ginsberg will chant and read with Gary Snyder, Michael McClure, and Lenore Kandel; Dick Alpert, Jerry Rubin, Dick Gregory, and Jack Weinberg will speak. Music will be played by all the Bay area rock bands, including the Grateful Dead, Big Brother and the Holding Company, Quicksilver Messenger Service, and many others. Everyone is invited to bring costumes, blankets, bells, flags, symbols, cymbals, drums, beads, feathers, flowers.

Now in the evolving generation of American young the humanization of the American man and woman can begin in joy and embrace without fear, dogma, suspicion or dialectical righteousness. A new concert of human relations being developed within the youthful underground must emerge, become conscious, and be shared so that a revolution of form can be filled with a Renaissance of compassion, awareness, and love in the Revelation of the unity of all mankind. The Human Be-In is the joyful, face-to-face beginning of the new epoch.

Article distributed with the Human Be-In press release.

Buddha passed around a basket of pot cookies to Jerry Rubin and the rest of the well-attended press conference.

Human Be-In poster by Rick Griffin.

149

Members of the tribes headed into Golden Gate Park and the Polo Fields for the Human Be-In.

The selection of the Polo Fields in Golden Gate Park for the Human Be-In came as the result of a conversation between Michael Bowen and a dope dealer known to the FBI as "John The Ghost." John had earned his alias one afternoon during a bust. Narcotics detectives had staked out his apartment, which was located in a converted single-residence house. The FBI also became involved with the case and assisted with his arrest. But when the cops started to come through the door, John, who has Mexican and Native American blood lines, eluded his pursuers by jumping out a window, grabbing an armful of newly-cut green shrubs along with a garden rake, then walked past police lines as the house gardener.

John used the Polo Fields as a place to exercise. With the success of the turnout for the Love Pageant Rally in the Panhandle, the expected attendance at the Be-In was estimated to exceed the 3,000 that packed the 666 event. John suggested to Bowen that the Polo Fields be used to hold the tribal event. Allen Cohen requested permission from the Parks Department to use the band shell across from the de Young Museum for the Be-In; but bad weather moved in, forcing the use of the Polo Fields. The decision to use the larger field was also based on the astrological findings of Ambrose Hollingsworth and Gavin Arthur.

Gavin Arthur, grandson of Chester Arthur, was a philosopher, writer, lecturer and astrologer who was approached to give his counsel in the selection of a date on which to hold the Human Be-In. Gavin lived in the Fillmore district on Buchanan Street. He thought well of the young people who came to him with increasing frequency from the Haight-Ashbury community. He also had contributed his writing to the *Oracle*. He announced January 14 as the day when communication and society would be most favored for a meld of positive communication for the greatest good. The date was also, he said, a time when the population of the earth would be equivalent in number to the total of all the dead in human history.

The letters of request for the Polo Fields were dispatched to the Parks Department's permit person, Peter Ash. In the fall of 1966 Peter Ash was a young attorney with the San Francisco Parks and Recreation Department. He had recently been promoted to Assistant Supervisor of Recreation.

Ash's responsibility was processing the dozens of park use requests that passed weekly over his desk. His office was in McLaren Lodge, the ivy covered stone administration office at the northeast corner of Golden Gate Park. On any given day Ash could look across Kennedy Drive or up Stanyan Street and see the Hashbury crazies headed into and out of the Park and its miles of quiet green seclusion. Until Ash became the giver of permissions, there had been an unofficial policy limiting the parks' open spaces to church and school groups. But Ash, a red-bearded thirty-three-year-old, had sympathy for the new lifestyle taking form outside his office windows. His park policy was to grant all requests for park use if at all possible. The parks were to be used by the public, he said. Reserving one of the park's vast green areas was a matter of a review of the request by the Park Department Board. The Park is enormous, three miles long, extending from the middle of the City to the shores of the Pacific Ocean. The Polo Fields alone could accommodate six square blocks of the Haight-Ashbury district into its spacious interior. Events of every description went on every week. During the summer solstice and the vernal equinox, strange religious rituals that included the occasional loss of a buffalo from the Buffalo Paddock strained Park officials who otherwise say that they maintained a "public first" philosophy.

The San Francisco Human Be-In begin in the Polo Fields at Golden Gate Park at noon on a sunny day.

January 14, 1967, was a clear winter day. We walked to the Be-In through the Park. Down paths marked with wind chimes, past gardens and lakes. Through the meadows. We were an army. Drawn to a great open field. Caught in a spell of anticipation. Giggling children. Happy people. Carrying flags and flowers and joy.

Poet Gary Snyder signaled the beginning of the Human Be-In by blowing a conch shell. Next to Snyder, Allen Ginsberg, chanted: "We are one! We are all one!"

The Be-In started with a blast from Gary Snyder's white-beaded conch shell. He blew long, mournful blasts which were lost on a crowd that stretched to the horizon. Drums and cymbals and tinkling bells broke into rhythm. Whistles and laughing. Singing and clapping. Hare-Krishna-Hare-Krishna-Hare-Hare-Hare-Rama-Hare-Rama-Rama-Rama-Hare-Hare. Allen Ginsberg, Michael McClure, Gary Snyder, Tim Leary, Michael Bowen, Lenore Kandel, Allen Cohen, Lawrence Ferlinghetti, Suzuki-Roshi. Ommmmmm. Clinking finger cymbals, clinking tambourines. "The God I worship is a lion." Dogs barked and wagged their tails and ran around. Someone blew a trumpet. Kids were lost and found. People laughed. The sun was warm. "Orange sunshine." Bands played. Flags waved. Walky-talky Chocolate George. A God's eye winked at the sun. Freewheeling Frank waved a tambourine. Dancing faces. Jerry Rubin got up and down. Leary tuned in and on and out. "Let it go, whatever you do is beautiful." People passed breads and cookies and grass and wine. Dennis Hopper made a film. When masked Steve the Gemini twin fell from the sky under a psychedelic parachute, everyone laughed and pointed and ooohhhed and aaahhhed. We were all lovers. The sun went down. "Peace in the heart, Dear. Peace in the Park here."

OMmmmmmm . . .

Hell's Angel Chocolate George took command of the Human Be-In security and helped return lost children.

Ron Thelin, poetess Lenore Kandel.

Kids were lost and found.

Tim Leary with yellow flowers tucked behind his ears chanted, "Turn on, tune in, drop out."

Left to right, Gary Snyder, Michael McClure, Allen Ginsberg, Freewheelin' Frank, Maretta.

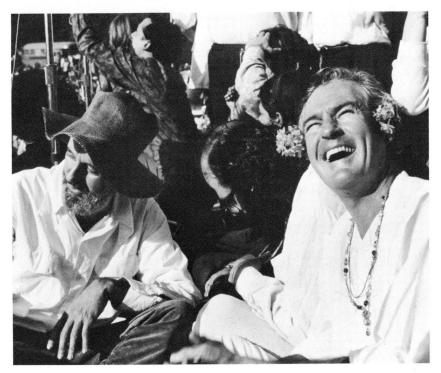

Poet Lawrence Ferlinghetti was invited to address the crowd but the power had been cut off, leaving the microphones dead. No matter, it was a memorable day.

By mid-afternoon the crowd on the Polo Fields had grown into an enormous gathering listening to the Quicksilver Messenger Service, the Jefferson Airplane and the Grateful Dead; poets recited poetry and hailed a new consciousness.

Then Allen Ginsberg
　　chanted a kitchen mantra.
　　　　"Sri Maitreya."
　　　　　　And the field was left clean.

"AND it is all perfect, this is really it.
  and IT is all perfect, this is really it.
    and it IS all perfect, this is really it.
      and it is ALL perfect, this is really it.
        and it is all PERFECT, this is really it.
          and it is all perfect, THIS is really it.
            and it is all perfect, this IS really it.
              and it is all perfect, this is REALLY it.
                and it is all perfect, this is really IT."

Excerpt from a poem by Michael McClure

After the Be-In, Michael Bowen hosted a party for some filmmakers at his studio. The guests included Allen Ginsberg, Tim Leary, and poet Gary Snyder.

"About eighteen people all in their Be-In costumes were snuggled into companionable heaps on the thin mattresses in Bowen's meditation room. Some of them were talking or chanting quietly to themselves. The others were staring amiably into space. They were all in the process of sharing a peace pipe, when Ginsberg and Maretta, tripping over a pile of people on the threshold, stumbled in. Maretta headed for a dark corner, where she staked out a few feet of mattress, curled up into a ball of culottes and fringe, and almost instantly fell asleep. Ginsberg located Snyder on a mattress behind the candelabra and sat down next to him. Snyder was wearing clothes—a pair of green corduroy jeans and a green blouse blocked with big mauve leaves and flowers—and waving around a gallon jug of California Bordeaux. Just as Ginsberg reached for the jug, a light went on, and two television men, dragging kliegs and cables, began maneuvering toward him. They said that Bowen had invited them. Ginsberg groaned.

"I don't know why, but this whole day strikes me as absolutely sane and right and beautiful," one of the men said cheerfully, holding a light meter up to Ginsberg's nose. "Mike must have put something in my tea last night."

"What's so insane about a little peace and harmony?" Ginsberg asked him, inching over on the mattress to make room for Maretta, who had been awakened by the light.

Maretta nodded sleepily, "It was fucking beautiful," she said.

"Like thousands of people would like to come to the park on a day like today," Ginsberg went on. "So they can relate to each other as—as dharma beings. All sorts of people. Poets, children, even Hell's Angels. People are lonesome. I'm lonesome. It's strange to be in a body. So what I'm doing—what we're all doing—on a day like today is saying, "Touch me, sleep with me, talk to me.""

"People are groovy," Snyder said.

"Zap!" Ginsberg said, and snapped his fingers. "You know how Reagan said, 'Once you've seen one redwood tree you've seen them all . . .'"

"That's an incredible mentality to us," Snyder broke in.

"Actually, I used to be in love with Reagan in the thirties—I used to see all his movies," Ginsberg said smiling ingenuously. "So Ronald Reagan and I are one. Ronald Reagan, you and I are one!"

Bowen, who had just come running into the room with a telephone in his hand, called to Ginsberg that he had Mexico on the line. "In Mexico, they meditated with us for six whole hours while we were at the Be-In," Bowen shouted as he leapt over a mattress, dropped down onto his hands and knees, and began tossing aside pillows until he located an extension socket in the wall.

"You mean to say you have a phone in your meditation room?" Ginsberg said, and burst out laughing.

"Hello, what's your name?" said Ginsberg, sticking a finger in his left ear. Ginsberg was talking to Bowen's guru in Mexico, John Cooke. "It's really far out here, man," said Ginsberg mimicking Bowen.

"Electric Tibet, baby," Bowen said, flipping Ginsberg the receiver. "Say something, will you Allen?"

"Hello, what's your name?" Ginsberg said, sticking a finger in his free ear. "Bright? Hey, that's a groovy name." Ginsberg turned to Snyder. "His name is Bright. That's nice." And then back to Mexico. "We're just saying that Ronald Reagan should prove his good faith by turning on."

"In the middle of the redwood forest, tell him," Snyder shouted.

Bowen reached for the phone. "It's really far out here, man," Bowen said.

Ginsberg peered at the television man, who was crawling around him with a long microphone cord in his hand.

"Take the phone call," Ginsberg told the television man. "It's like we're bridging the gap between all sorts of people with this—this kind of community festival. I thought it was very Eden-like today, actually. Kind of like Blake's vision of Eden. Music. Babies. People just sort of floating around having a good time and everybody happy and smiling and touching and turning each other on and a lot of groovy chicks all dressed up in their best clothes and—"

"But will it *last?*" the television man said.

Ginsberg shrugged, "How do *I* know if it will last?" he said. "And if it doesn't turn out, who cares?"

"Acid just happened to turn up as the product of this particular society, to correct its own excesses."

Gary Snyder

Excerpted from *Allen Ginsberg in America* by Jane Kramer

Outside on the street in front of Bowen's place, the cops had set up road blocks to prevent traffic entering the Haight. The police said that "the commotion began about 9 P.M. after the hippies returned from a giant 'happening' [Be-In] at Golden Gate Park that lasted until dusk. High on LSD," the story continues, "the hippies gathered in the 1500 block of Haight Street and obstructed three buses and cars. Then pushed people off the walks. About forty hippies who refused to disperse were loaded into four paddy wagons. Twenty-five people were locked up at Park Station and charged with creating a nuisance."

A great butterfly had emerged and taken wing in the setting sun of the San Francisco Human Be-In. It flew across the land, then on across the seas to other continents. Wherever that psychedelic butterfly touched down to earth its spirit captured the consciousness of masses of young people. Its being so influenced those that were touched by it that the essence became the life force of a revolution. A nonviolent revolution had begun. Twenty thousand people had rallied in celebration of a new spirit of consciousness. That fact caused a considerable stir. The social and political implications divided large numbers of people at a time when the war in Vietnam had already badly shaken the country. The Haight-Ashbury and the Human Be-In scared some people and for others it became an inspiration. For the rest of 1967 and into the 1970s the Haight-Ashbury attracted tens of thousands of kids and influenced millions more. The potential of the human spirit had been recognized and it would be tested by youth for generations to come.

Where have all the flowers gone?

On October 6, 1967, the Diggers and hundreds of Haight-Ashbury flower folk celebrated the last hippie event, "The Death of Hippie." There was a parade and a ceremony that concluded with a burial of the Psychedelic Shop store sign. The Thelin brothers quit the Hashbury and were followed soon after by Michael Bowen, Emmett Grogan, Allen Cohen and others. Bowen headed south for Mexico, but returned briefly in 1968 to aid in the march on the Pentagon. Michael and his friend, Bill Fortner, purchased a half-ton of daisies to distribute over the Pentagon from an airplane, but the FBI stopped them before they could take flight, and the flowers were trucked to the picket line at the military headquarters. There the daisies were photographed by the world press protruding from the muzzles of rifles held by the troops guarding the Pentagon. The Army had accomplished what the hippies could not; in order to keep the hippies out, the soldiers had surrounded the building.

The general exodus from the Haight started with the original prime movers. Bowen settled into a painter's life in Mexico; Allen Cohen moved in with a communal group in northern California to write; Emmett Grogan took up residence in New York City, where he wrote a novel and shortly thereafter died. Chocolate George met his end in a traffic accident on Haight Street; Chet Helms created a new rock concert venue with the Tribal Stomps; Phyllis Willner became a nurse and still lives in San Francisco. Michael McClure commutes to world capitals, arranging for productions of his plays and publication of his books. Timothy Leary is a stand-up comic on the night club circuit; Stewart Brand turned to publishing, with *The Whole Earth Catalogue* and the *Co-Evolutionary Quarterly;* Bill Graham became the paragon of rock concert producers; the Grateful Dead continue to beguile their fans; the Charlatans split up and George Hunter became a designer. "Mouse" and Alton Kelley create rock concert posters; Bill Ham continues to explore new dimensions of light and color; Ken Kesey moved back to his ancestral farm near Eugene, Oregon, to write another book, and Allen Ginsberg and Gary Snyder continue their careers writing, lecturing, and traveling the world. Today the buildings that housed the Fillmore and Winterland stand unused and empty. The Avalon has become a movie theater, and Haight Street is sprouting boutiques, coffee houses, and restaurants.

The Dance Concerts 🎵

Music kept the beat. The concerts and the ballrooms
provided a place to get together. The village well.
To prove that they were real.

BILL GRAHAM'S DANCE CONCERTS

At the Calliope Warehouse

1965

NOVEMBER 6—APPEAL 1
Jefferson Airplane
Fugs
Sandy Bull
John Handy Quintet
The Committee
Lawrence Ferlinghetti
and others.
(BENEFIT FOR THE SAN FRANCISCO
MIME TROUPE)

At the Fillmore Auditorium

DECEMBER 10—APPEAL II
Jefferson Airplane
Great Society
John Handy Quintet
Mystery Trend
Gentlemen's Band
(BENEFIT FOR THE SAN FRANCISCO
MIME TROUPE)

1966

JANUARY 14—APPEAL III
Great Society
Mystery Trend
Grateful Dead
Gentlemen's Band
(BENEFIT FOR THE SAN FRANCISCO
MIME TROUPE)

FEBRUARY 4, 5 and 6
Jefferson Airplane
Mystery Trend
and others.

MARCH 18
Mystery Trend
Big Brother & the
   Holding Company
The Family Tree

MARCH 19
Quicksilver Messenger Service
Family Tree
Gentlemen's Band

MARCH 20
Quicksilver Messenger Service
Great Society
Skins

MARCH 25, 26 and 27
Butterfield Blues Band
Quicksilver Messenger Service

APRIL 3
Invaders
V.I.P.'s
Freddy & The Stone Souls

APRIL 7
Russian Poet Andrei Voznesensky
Jefferson Airplane

APRIL 15, 16 and 17
Butterfield Blues Band
Jefferson Airplane

APRIL 22 and 23
Grass Roots
Quicksilver Messenger Service
Family Tree

APRIL 29 and 30
Jefferson Airplane
Quicksilver Messenger Service
Lightnin' Hopkins

MAY 6 and 7
Jefferson Airplane
The Jaywalkers

MAY 13 and 14
New Generation
The Jaywalkers
The Charlatans

MAY 20 and 21
Quicksilver Messenger Service
The Final Solution

MAY 237, 28 and 29
Andy Warhol & his Plastic Inevitable
Velvet Underground
Nico
The Mothers of Invention

JUNE 3 and 4
Quicksilver Messenger Service
Grateful Dead
The Mothers of Invention

JUNE 10 and 11
Jefferson Airplane
Great Society
Heavenly Blues Band

JUNE 17 and 18
Wailers
Quicksilver Messenger Service

JUNE 23
Them
New Tweedy Brothers

JUNE 24 and 25
Lenny Bruce
The Mothers of Invention

JULY 1
Quicksilver Messenger Service
Big Brother & the
   Holding Company
The Jaywalkers

JULY 2
Great Society
Sopwith Camel
The Charlatans

JULY 3
Love
Grateful Dead
Group B

JULY 6
Turtles
Oxford Circle

JULY 8 and 9
Mindbenders
Chocolate Watchband

JULY 15, 16 and 17
Jefferson Airplane
Grateful Dead

JULY 17
Poet Allen Ginsberg
Sopwith Camel
The Committee
The San Francisco Mime Troupe
and others
(BENEFIT A.R.T.S.)

JULY 22
Association
Quicksilver Messenger Service
Grassroots

JULY 23
Association
Quicksilver Messenger Service
Sopwith Camel

JULY 24
A stage play, "The Beard,"
by Michael McClure

JULY 29 and 30
Them
Sons of Champlin

AUGUST 5 and 6
Love
Everpresent Fullness

AUGUST 7
Quicksilver Messenger Service
Big Brother & the
   Holding Company
Grateful Dead
Grassroots
Sunshine
The Committee
The San Francisco Mime Troupe
The Jook Savages
PH Factor
(BENEFIT FOR CHILDREN'S ADVENTURE
DAY CAMP)

AUGUST 10
Sam the Sham and the Pharaohs
The Sit-ins

AUGUST 12 and 13
Jefferson Airplane
Grateful Dead

AUGUST 17
Jefferson Airplane
Quicksilver Messenger Service
Mimi Farina
The Only Alternative and his
   Other Possibility

AUGUST 19 and 20
Young Rascals
Quicksilver Messenger Service

AUGUST 26 and 27
Thirteenth Floor Elevators
Great Society
Sopwith Camel

SEPTEMBER 2 and 3
Jefferson Airplane
PH Factor Jugband
Andrew Staples

SEPTEMBER 4
Grateful Dead
Quicksilver Messenger Service
Country Joe & the Fish

SEPTEMBER 5
Martha & the Vandellas
Johnny Talbot & De Thangs

SEPTEMBER 9 and 10
The Mothers of Invention
Oxford Circle
(Due to a religious ceremony at the
synagogue next to the Fillmore, the
concert was moved to the Scottish
Rite Temple across town.)

SEPTEMBER 11
Concerned Negro voter registration
rally—various artists

SEPTEMBER 11
Jon Hendricks Trio
Elvin Jones
Joe Henderson Quartet
Big Mama Thornton
Denny Zeitlin Trio
Jefferson Airplane
Great Society
Wildflower
(BENEFIT FOR THE BOTH/AND JAZZ CLUB)

SEPTEMBER 16 and 17
The Byrds
Wildflower
A stage play, "The Dutchman,"
by Leroi Jones

SEPTEMBER 23, 24, 25, 30 and
OCTOBER 1 and 2
Jefferson Airplane
Butterfield Blues Band
Muddy Waters

OCTOBER 7, 8 and 9
Butterfield Blues Band
Jefferson Airplane
Grateful Dead

OCTOBER 14, 15 and 16
Butterfield Blues Band
Jefferson Airplane
Big Mama Thornton

OCTOBER 20
Manitas de Plata

OCTOBER 21 and 22
Grateful Dead
Lightnin' Hopkins
Loading Zone

OCTOBER 23
Yardbirds
Country Joe & the Fish

OCTOBER 28, 29 and 30
Captain Beef Heart & his Magic Band
Chocolate Watchband
Great Pumpkin

NOVEMBER 4, 5 and 6
Muddy Waters
Quicksilver Messenger Service
Andrew Staples

NOVEMBER 6
Jefferson Airplane and others

NOVEMBER 11, 12 and 13
Bola Sete
Country Joe & the Fish
Buffalo Springfield

NOVEMBER 18, 19 and 20
Grateful Dead
James Cotton Blues Band
Lothar & the Hand People.

NOVEMBER 20
Quicksilver Messenger Service
James Cotton Blues Band
Grateful Dead
John Talbot and De Thangs
(BENEFIT FOR STUDENT NON-VIOLENT
COORDINATING COMMITTEE)

NOVEMBER 25, 26 and 27
Jefferson Airplane
James Cotton Blues Band
Moby Grape

CHET HELMS' FAMILY DOG DANCE CONCERTS

DECEMBER 2, 3 and 4
Love
Moby Grape
Lee Michaels

DECEMBER 9, 10 and 11
Grateful Dead
Big Mama Thornton
Tim Rose

DECEMBER 16, 17 and 18
Jefferson Airplane
Junior Wells Chicago Blues Band
Tim Rose

DECEMBER 20
Otis Redding
Grateful Dead

DECEMBER 21
Otis Redding
Johnny Talbot & De Thangs

DECEMBER 22
Otis Redding
Country Joe & the Fish

DECEMBER 30
Jefferson Airplane
Grateful Dead
Quicksilver Messenger Service

AT WINTERLAND

NEW YEAR'S EVE, 1966-'67
Jefferson Airplane
Grateful Dead
Quicksilver Messenger Service
(9 P.M. to 9 A.M. with breakfast)

1967

JANUARY 6, 7 and 8
Young Rascals
Sopwith Camel
The Doors

JANUARY 13, 14 and 15
Grateful Dead
Junior Wells
Chicago Blues Band
The Doors

1966

At the Fillmore Auditorium

FEBRUARY 19
Jefferson Airplane
Big Brother and the
   Holding Company

FEBRUARY 26
King Kong Memorial Dance
The Great Society
Grass Roots
Big Brother and the
   Holding Company
Quicksilver Messenger Service

MARCH 25, 26 and 27
Paul Butterfield Blues Band
Quicksilver Messenger Service

APRIL 8 and 9
The Love
The Sons of Adam
The Charlatans
Lights by Tony Martin

At the Avalon Ballroom

APRIL 22 and 23
The Blues Project
The Great Society
Lights and stuff by Tony Martin

MAY 6 and 7
The Daily Flash
The Rising Sons
Big Brother and the
   Holding Company
The Charlatans
Lights by Bill Ham

MAY 13 and 14
The Blues Project
The Sons of Adam
Quicksilver Messenger Service
Lights by Bill Ham

MAY 20, 21 and 22
Hupmobile-8
The Love
Captain Beef Heart and
   His Magic Band
Big Brother and the
   Holding Company

MAY 27 and 28
Grass Roots
The Grateful Dead

JUNE 3 and 4
Grass Roots
Big Brother and the
   Holding Company
The Buddha from Muir Beach

JUNE 10 and 11
The Grateful Dead
Quicksilver Messenger Service
The New Tweedy Brothers

JUNE 17 and 18
Captain Beef Heart and
   His Magic Band
Big Brother and
   the Holding Company

JUNE 24 and 25
Big Brother and
   the Holding Company
Quicksilver Messenger Service
Lights by Bill Ham

JULY 1, 2 and 3
Grass Roots
Daily Flash
Sopwith Camel
Lights by Bill Ham

JULY 8, 9 and 10
Sir Douglas Quintet
Ever Present Fullness
Lights by Bill Ham

JULY 22 and 23
Jefferson Airplane
The Great Society
Lights by Bill Ham

JULY 28, 29 and 30
Bo Diddley
Quicksilver Messenger Service
Lights by Bill Ham

AUGUST 5 and 6
Big Brother and the
   Holding Company
The Oxford Circle
Bo Diddley
The Sons of Adam
Lights by Bill Ham

AUGUST 12 and 13
Bo Diddley
Big Brother and the
   Holding Company
Lights by Bill Ham

AUGUST 19 and 20
The Grateful Dead
Sopwith Camel
Lights by Bill Ham

AUGUST 26 and 27
Captain Beef Heart and
   His Magic Band
The Charlatans

SEPTEMBER 2 and 3
Thirteen Floor Elevators
Sir Douglas Quintet

SEPTEMBER 9 and 10
Quicksilver Messenger Service
The Great Society

SEPTEMBER 16 and 17
The Grateful Dead
The Oxford Circle

SEPTEMBER 30 and October 1
Thirteen Floor Elevators
Quicksilver Messenger Service

OCTOBER 7 and 8
Jim Kweskin Jug Band
The Electric Train
Big Brother and the
   Holding Company

OCTOBER 15 and 16
Big Brother and the
   Holding Company
Sir Douglas Quintet

OCTOBER 21 and 22
The Daily Flash
Country Joe and the Fish

OCTOBER 28 and 29
Quicksilver Messenger Service
Blackburn & Snow
Sons of Champlin

NOVEMBER 11 and 12
Thirteen Floor Elevators
Moby Grape

NOVEMBER 18 and 19
The Daily Flash
Quicksilver Messenger Service
Country Joe and the Fish

NOVEMBER 25 and 26
Quicksilver Messenger Service
Big Brother and the
   Holding Company
Country Joe and the Fish

DECEMBER 2 and 3
Buffalo Springfield
The Daily Flash
Congress of Wonders

DECEMBER 9 and 10
The Oxford Circle
Big Brother and the
   Holding Company
Lee Michaels

DECEMBER 16 and 17
Young Bloods
Sparrow
Sons of Champlin

DECEMBER 23 and 24
The Grateful Dead

DECEMBER 30 and 31
Country Joe and the Fish
Moby Grape
Lee Michaels

HAIGHT-ASHBURY FAREWELL
(Sung to the tune of *Red River Valley*)

From this city they say you are going . . .
I am sorry you feel you must flee
But remember your friends who were hippies
And stayed in the Haight-Ashbury.

Chorus

So come sit in the park one more hour
It was here you first opened your mind
And in friendship I'll give you a flower
To remind you of love left behind.

Oh, I hear you've been talking of justice.
Of improving the world and all men,
But I tell you that world is a circle
Leading back to yourself once again.

If you love this old world and wish truly
To improve it before you are dead,
You don't have to press others unduly
Better start with the world inside your head.

From a lyric by anonymous Haight-Ashbury composer

Index

Hippie

The derivation of hippie *precedes Elizabethan England. The term was used in English country wrestling, a stand-up sport with the contest concluding when any part of the body touched the ground. The vengeful moneylender, Shylock, in Shakespeare's* The Merchant of Venice, *speaks of Antonio: "If I can catch him once upon the hip, I will feed fat the ancient grudge I bear him." And in the last act: "Now, Infidel, I have you on the hip." A contestant that won at English wrestling was said to be "hip." During the Swing era of jazz in the 1930s,* hip *and* hep *were interchanged when people became* hipped *on the new rhythms. In the 1940s, Cab Calloway was characterized as "Mr. Hip" and he wrote a Hipster's Dictionary. Webster's New International Dictionary of the English Language defines* hipped *as a colloquial adjective: 1. Depressed; low-spirited, and having one's interest unreasonably centered; obsessed.* Hippy *is defined as a hypochondriac.*